COMFORT ZONE CORRECTION

Unfiltered True Stories in Successful Selling

EMILY HORABIK

Printed in the United States of America

ISBN 978-0-578-60954-6

Contributors:

Dr. Dave Downey
Professor Emeritus Center for Food and Agricultural Business Purdue University, West Lafayette, IN
www.agribusiness.purdue.edu/faculty-and-staff/david-downey

VEER© Diamonds and Strategies
31 W 47th St Suite 702 New York, NY 10036
www.veer.diamonds

Legal Team: Law Office of Sejal Rajan, PLLC Intellectual Property Law
860 Willis Avenue #31 Albertson, NY 11507
Law@SejalRajan.com

Edited by Amy Dupcak & Susan Ratliff

Designed by Brandi Hollister, Hollister Design Group

ACKNOWLEDGEMENTS

I want to sincerely thank everyone who
helped make the recollection of these experiences
possible and to everyone who contributed
to the success of this project.

I would especially like to thank
Dr. Dave Downey of Purdue University
who took the time to give this book structure
and help us in making this dream project a success.

TABLE OF CONTENTS

HOW TO USE THIS BOOK

Have you ever thought of yourself as an entrepreneur? Let me tell you that most individuals are entrepreneurs, the only difference is the level of entrepreneurship. It's so sad to see that so many people know their full potential and capabilities yet fail to act upon them. These people feel stuck in a routine. Are you working in circles but not getting results?

You are not alone. I had the same problem. I doubted whether I could break the routine I had created over the years until I met my mentor. This book is a collection of my mentor's real-life experiences that helped him to attain his desired dream. It was not easy. It took a lot of work, courage and sacrifice. He made a lot of mistakes but kept moving toward his dream.

- Feel free to read this book from cover to cover in one sitting. You can also read a story daily and slowly incorporate those lessons into your day to day life.
- The questions at the beginning of each chapter will warm up your mind and get you ready for the lessons you are about to discover through each circumstance.
- The Wrap Ups Lessons highlight each chapter's encounter and can be used as a guide.
- You may come across a similar situation in the future, analyze and decide what you would have done differently. Do something that moves you forward instead of keeping you in your safety net. Even if you are happy where you are in your job and you're just interested in reading about a fellow go-getter's experience, you will surely learn something.

I am telling these true-life experiences to my best recollection. I have included the location and year the event took place, when relevant. The only thing I have changed are the names of the other parties involved in the stories in respect for their privacy.

Each chapter will show you why it is important to always try to be different. You may not come across the same experience, but you will learn why being different draws attention, wins customers and creates growth in any industry. No matter what adversity one faces, or how low on the totem pole one starts, all you need is a little grit to take that first step and make it over the future hurdles that may come.

Let this book be your wake-up call to come out from the Comfort Zone, remind you to recollect your passion and dreams and go after them. Success is always possible, even if you have failed previously. This book is proof of that.

CHAPTER

1

DOMESTICATED BEAST

DOMESTICATED BEAST

"Domestication is a dream crusher." – Mr. Brown

You have been domesticated. Yes, we human beings are nearly the same as domesticated animals like dogs and cats, or tigers or lions at the zoo. Sounds crazy but it is so true. Think about it. When was the last time you had to go out and search for food? Now we have it nicely packaged at the grocery store... down the street... that we drive to. When was the last time you had to walk very far to find water? Most people have running water and even toilets in their homes. We have become domesticated.

If you sit back and observe any pet being raised, you will see they are given everything they need by their human. In domestication, they are not afraid of survival. They live in comfort. Now, put them in the wild and it will be a very different story. We humans have also gotten used to this idea of living comfortably. I'm sure you want to achieve your dreams without any discomfort as well, but we all know this is wishful thinking.

I believe most human beings born in this world are born with a dream to do something with their life. Maybe you start working an entry level job in a bank and strive to someday be the President of said bank. Maybe you begin work as a mail clerk and want to work your way up. Maybe you start working as a chef in hopes of one day opening your own restaurant. The possibilities are endless. However, once you start working and begin to get a paycheck, this very silly paycheck puts you into a Comfort Zone. You think, huh, I can pursue my own dreams next week. Soon, you get sucked into day to day challenges that would make you uncomfortable if you did not have this paycheck. Maybe it's rent, a mortgage, a car or a vacation. With the paycheck, life gets comfortable. Your domestication makes you forget about what you really wanted to do with your life. You forget why you initially started that job as the checks keep rolling in. You don't realize you are working for someone else's dream. Your dream starts to become just a dream, then quickly a distant possible reality.

Does this scenario sound familiar? You are not alone! Maybe your coworkers, your family or friends are also complacent. You need not take the easy route. Find that little bit of wild that is still roaring deep inside you and get up and out of your Comfort Zone! Your dreams are not just dreams! They have the potential to become reality with the right work ethic at any age! No one is going to come up to you and hand you your dream. You must work for it. Working smart and working hard are two of the most important ingredients in acquiring your dream. A little luck is the third. See challenges as mere hurdles. Stay focused and determined. Success will follow.

Let's imagine a young boy who never let himself become domesticated. He would go to and from school, eat his dinner, finish his homework and take a walk towards his dream in the evening. Every single day he would walk over a mile until he reached the public viewing gallery of the airport where he would watch the planes take off and land. With every single plane that ascended into the sky, his desire and intensity to fly away to a distant land grew stronger. He was becoming tired of the day to day grind to survive. By his twenties, he had tried his hand at a few jobs from selling soap door to door to going to law school, realizing these professions were not what he wanted. He refused to settle for just a good job. He had a burning desire to do something he had yet to find and he let himself listen to it. His every breath and step were leading him towards his dream.

Sure enough, one day this man took off to the land of opportunities, The United States of America. He landed in New York City, where he thought the sky's the limit. He soon realized he had a lot to learn in this new land and new culture when he started applying for work. On his first attempt to get a job, he walked up to a gas station on High Ridge Road in Stamford, CT and asked if they were hiring. The owner asked, “Do you know how to pump gas?” The young man had no car, didn’t know how to drive, and had absolutely no idea how to fill up a gas tank. When the owner said, “I will call you,” our naive young man was ecstatic to have gotten a job in such a short amount of time. He did not realize that in this new land this was the opposite. It was a polite way of saying you did NOT get the job.

His next stop was to the brand-new Stamford Town Centre. He applied for a job at JCPenney and was interviewed by the personnel manager. Mr. York seemed to like the eager man’s hunger for a job when he explained during the interview, “I am new here. If you show me how to sell a stone from the street, I can sell a stone.” This answer was one Mr. York had never heard before and got him into the next string of interviews. This young man had no experience and most of the department managers were hesitant to hire someone so FOB (Fresh Off the Boat). However, the Men’s Dept Manager Mr. Buck Harris liked the answer. He decided to take a gamble on him. The young man was in! He had his first American job at $3.65 an hour which was minimum wage back then.

The retail job lasted only until 4:30 p.m. and the newcomer wanted to make the most of his time. There were still so many hours left in the day! What kind of place could he work at that was open at night? A fast food restaurant was the answer, more specifically the Burger King on High Ridge Road in Stamford. He found himself with the same dilemma as before, no experience, and add to that he was vegetarian. He had never eaten a hamburger, let alone cooked one! Even though he did not know the difference between mayonnaise and tartar sauce, he talked himself into a position at

$3.75 an hour. The money started flowing and he became one step closer to his dream.

He was excited to work and learn. He would work from 8 a.m. to 4:30 p.m. at JCPenney and then 7 p.m. to midnight at Burger King. Having two different jobs in two different industries helped him adapt to the new land and culture. Retail taught him how to fine tune his personality to sell effectively, how to communicate with American mannerisms, and how to work slang into his sentences. Burger King taught him that no work is inferior. Cleaning the kitchen, dining tables and bathrooms was no problem if it was taking him one step closer to his goal. For him, no work was below a person's dignity. It solidified a work ethic in him that he still maintains to this day.

This went on for well over two years, but at $3.65 and $3.75 an hour, how far towards the sky can you go? A dynamic businessman from overseas, who had kept in touch with the young man after his move, decided to take a gamble on him. The businessman was in the diamond industry, a business where trust is everything. Our young man found himself starting a business from the ground up. His dream was really starting to take shape. He had finally found his calling.

When he first started his business venture, he did not have any money for an office or a phone, so he needed to be creative for people to take him seriously. When he was not working his other jobs, he would go into the city from Connecticut and arrive in Grand Central Station. There, he would exchange $5 into dimes and make cold calls from a payphone booth. It had sliding doors and a seat where you could sit down for privacy. Without paying a dime in rent for his makeshift office, he was in the lower level of Rockefeller Center Plaza with his own business. Every phone call would cost a dime. He was making 50 phone calls a day to sell his diamonds. Most calls would be met with "We will call you back, what is your telephone number?" He would reply simply, "I will give you a call again tomorrow." Gradually, he started building up a client base and upgraded from phone booth to small office space.

Though things were picking up, he continued working at Burger King at night and JCPenney on the weekends. Imagine all the commuting! He did what he had to do to make sure his bills were paid. Eventually, to the dismay of both his managers, he got the guts to take the next scary step forward to work solely for his own business full time. He had arrived at his dream, ready to do what it took to stay there.

My dear reader, please allow me to introduce this young man as Mr. Brown, my mentor whom I have written this book about. He is proof that the initial uncomfortable sacrifice that you make early in life always pays off in the long run. I had the pleasure of meeting this man through my dear friend and old roommate Kow. Mr. Brown and Kow worked alongside each other for years before Kow decided to venture off on his own and create his own company named VEER©. We decided to share our mentor's non-fiction personal life experiences for this very reason. Think of these stories as your mentorship to help you attain your dream.

Keep in mind that these lessons are applicable to any of life's situations, not just entrepreneurship. Maybe you are trying to get to a starting position on a sports team. Maybe you are trying to cook a full meal instead of just snacks. Maybe you are working the reception desk at a hotel and one day you wish to own your own. Maybe you begin a career as a financial analyst at an investment firm with an eye to be at the top of the firm. Maybe you are trying to teach your dog new tricks. No matter the situation, it is human nature to settle into the Comfort Zone. You may think, hey this is enough, I can settle for this. But think how much happier you can be if you take the risk to push yourself forward. Think about the pride you will feel running the first play of the game. Think how satisfied you will be when you serve your first three course homemade meal and then become a world-renowned chef. Think about how happy you will be walking through the door of your hotel you created. Think about that view from the top of the firm. Think about when your dog can walk with you off the leash and still listen to everything you say. These dreams are achievable when you challenge yourself and break yourself out of the Comfort Zone.

THE WRAP UPS – BY MR. BROWN

- *Keep adapting until you find the right fit.*
- *You must try to win.*
- *Even a small boat can catch numerous fish.*

CHAPTER

2

WHY MR. BROWN?

Would you work with someone who is boring?

WHY MR. BROWN?

"Laugh, even at your own expense." – Mr. Brown

You may wonder how my mentor's nickname Mr. Brown came into existence. This is *the* story that gave my mentor his infamous nickname Mr. Brown.

New York, New York - Holiday Season

It was 2008. The economy in the USA and all around the world was shaky. My mentor's business was no exception to this changing environment. However, instead of just thinking about how to keep his own head above water and keep his doors open, he saw this as a challenge and an opportunity to grow business. The sales team constantly brainstormed about sales and marketing strategies, how to grow business and how to prevent their clients from sliding away from their own business goals. My mentor strived to work alongside them as a united front against the circumstances of the economy. Remember, Mr. Brown believes one's baby business is nothing without its' nourishment and he reminds his clients of this as well.

Instead of making sales phone calls, which clients admitted they were starting to dread, one genius from his sales team said, "How about putting your face in an ad?" They knew when the clients would come across the ad they would laugh at the expression on my mentor's face. To add more humor, below the picture of his face, they would list the various pieces of jewelry being promoted with the phrase, "What can this Mr. Brown do for you?" They saw this as an excellent way to connect with the audience that they were trying to reach and grab the attention of existing clients with the help of a good laugh. At this point the nickname "Mr. Brown" was born.

The team went into the fall and holiday season of that year excited to win big and anxious to see where the ad would lead. The moment clients recognized Mr. Brown's face in the picture on the upper right-hand corner of the website, their first reaction was, *what is this guy doing here?* As they scrolled down, they got such a kick out of the token phrase, as well as Mr. Brown's face. He did not like being in pictures so when people saw his face it was a shocker. Clients not only laughed out loud, but most of them called the office to tell them of their good laugh. The creative gamble was a hit! Dreaded phone calls were replaced by phones ringing off the hook with clients calling in wanting the advertised merchandise. The ad was so successful that every item that was promoted received a tremendous sales boost. Business interactions became fun and as they chatted, the size of each existing order grew. That strategy resulted in a huge increase to their sales volume!

The goal of getting attention and closing a bunch of new clients was accomplished. Some of these new clients were the very clients who hadn't even given them an opportunity to present their products in the past. Now, they were not only calling and speaking with the sales team but placing sample orders for pieces they could inspect in person.

By the time the spring tradeshows rolled around, Mr. Brown's name was forgotten and he was recognized only as "Mr. Brown." At tradeshows, firms mingle with each other and discuss various problems they are facing in their businesses. They also share their holiday season experiences in meetings and team clinics, including how they increased sales or ways they were able to maintain the same level of sales as the previous year. Since the USA was still in recession, everyone was in the same rocky boat as the rest of the country. Many of the firms that had worked with Mr. Brown during that holiday season spoke openly about his face being part of the ad. Some of the clients who failed to capitalize on these promotions felt guilty that they had missed out on a trip in Mr. Brown's boat that had made many of his client's decent amounts of money. They came up to Mr. Brown's firm during the spring show saying how they had heard great things about him, his team, and the quality of the items they had promoted. New customers were also lining up to see Mr. Brown's ad merchandise right then and there in person. The ad, through word of mouth, continued to bring in sales long after it was taken down. It just goes to show how adding a small touch of humor can go a long way.

Even now when clients call the office on business, the first question they ask is how is the notorious Mr. Brown doing and is he free to speak for a moment? He has officially lost his given name. He doesn't take it personally but sees the humor in it and uses it to his advantage! After reading in between the lines when speaking with lots of his clients, many were under a lot of stress and pressure. In addition, they were constantly conducting bland business meetings. If anyone could make a stressed client feel better, make some of their moments cheerful, or fill a few moments of their life with a little fun, humor and laughter, an everlasting impression will be made upon them. They will most likely look forward to your phone calls. Mr. Brown likes to quote his friend Todd from Statesville, North Carolina, who rightly said, "Never take life too seriously. Nobody has come out of it alive yet."

THE WRAP UPS – BY MR. BROWN

- *Laughter may earn you a nickname. Learn how to cash it out.*
- *Humor exists in all situations, even during a recession.*
- *Do not be afraid to take a low stakes gamble and try something new. Agree to a challenge within your boundaries.*

UNIVERSITY OF MR. BROWN

Do you have the freedom to be yourself?

UNIVERSITY OF MR. BROWN

"The business is your baby and the customer is its food and nutrients." – Mr. Brown

---

I want to devote this chapter to my friend Kow, who was willing to share his mentor, Mr. Brown, with me. I can count on one hand the number of people I have met in my life that possess the same amount of energy that Kow and I have. I can't explain it, but it's like we can never shut off. And if we are in the same room, forget about it, good luck keeping up with us. The moment Mr. Brown started talking at our first encounter over coffee, I saw immediately why Kow had chosen him as a mentor. He was one of us! He had been able to focus his energy into a very specific mentality that Kow and I were both struggling with! I could not think of a better mentor to learn from and I am extremely thankful to them both for letting me into their circle of trust. The energy was high as they began to tell me all about their mutual love of their businesses and about how they met.

Kow arrived in the United States in December of 2000, the millennium year, for postgraduate study. College taught him about American mannerisms, culture, discipline, freedom, behavior, and above all, how to project confidence. When he graduated, it was with this newfound confidence that he decided to move to New York City to work for a large jewelry manufacturing company. He was one of the few students from his school with a job lined up after graduation. He wondered if the stars had aligned in his horoscope and if New York was his destiny.

He soon got bored with his job because it was monotonous and there was no action in managing the marketing and print media for such a huge jewelry firm. He was just not learning anything new. He was just another number in a sea of employees he could learn nothing from. He wanted more interaction with the actual customer. He found himself looking for another opportunity where he would be able to expand his horizon and put his knowledge into practice. After conducting some research about Mr. Brown's firm, Kow thought that place could be his dream job. Here was a growing business with lots of action that was gaining traction and momentum in the industry. That was precisely what my friend was looking for. A place that could really ignite the fire in his blood.

Kow was in. Mr. Brown kept a close eye on him during his probationary year wanting to be sure of Kow's potential before he would invest time and energy into the newbie. Though he didn't trust him wholeheartedly in the beginning, he was always quick to guide Kow in his follies. Keep in mind, Mr. Brown was working on expanding a successful jewelry business that he'd built from the ground up, and Kow was just a twenty-two-year-old with a lot to learn.

Kow looked up to his new boss who had also immigrated to America and started from scratch. He jumped at the chance to brainstorm new ideas with Mr. Brown whenever the opportunity presented itself, which led Mr. Brown to see something brewing in Kow. He had the same hunger Mr. Brown possessed and few others experienced. Around two years into the job Mr. Brown invited Kow to lunch. He remembers it vividly. He loves to tell the story of his first lunch with Mr. Brown. I even remember what they had: boiled carrots, broccoli, and radish, served with some toasted slices of sprouted grain bread from Trader Joe's, accompanied by all-natural sweetened jelly from Polaner and hot Tetley Tea. It was not a spectacular feast, but it was the best meal of Kow's life. I remember how proud he was that he'd finally been admitted into his mentor's confidence, aka The University of Mr. Brown.

Kow was ecstatic to have a mentor who took the time to personally teach him about thinking beyond the four walls of the box. His mentor was all about the customer and nothing but the customer. What a concept. Kow found himself learning new strategies from his mentor every day. All team members had the freedom to be themselves without any filters. Kow was so excited to be working with customers, that every time he satisfied a customer beyond their dreams, he would stand up and clap at his desk unable to contain how full he was of customer satisfaction. It's perhaps not surprising that his fellow team members didn't approve of his behavior. He'd often get a roll of the eye but who the heck cared? He'd been accepted into The University of Mr. Brown, where the freedom to be yourself was one of the perks.

There was only one rule and one rule alone: one must always take care of their customer and the business. The business is the baby and the customer is its food and nutrients. Without good nutrition, the baby will not grow.

The only lesson to be mastered was how to take care of your customer. Eventually, Kow graduated and created a company of his own named VEER© based on his degree of education from The University Of Mr. Brown. His company follows these same ground rules to this day.

THE WRAP UPS – BY MR. BROWN

- *Surround yourself with positive motivators.*
- *Keep moving forward. Do not lose momentum.*
- *Stand up and clap for yourself when you have earned it.*

Kow is a nickname bestowed upon Kaushal Shah by Mr. Brown.
Many industry friends lovingly call him Kow.

Kaushal runs a solution driven business under the banner
VEER© Diamonds and Strategies.

Learn more about how to grow your business,
increase market share and profit
with VEER© programs and strategies at
www.veer.diamonds
or give Kow a call at 855-836-5483.

Has money ever fallen in your lap?

Have you ever sold a product but did not get paid?

Did you ever think of a bathroom as a conference room?

Have you ever been ticketed for a traffic violation?

Have you ever lost money in the stock market?

Are you content with what you get?

Let's get answers to some of the above questions from Mr. Brown's encounters during Trade Show Events.

TRADE SHOW EXPERIENCES

There are thousands of trade shows, expos, seminars and conventions taking place in various industries each year across America. Multiply those thousands by the number of exhibitors in each of those places. You will arrive at numbers that are staggering and run into the millions.

Trade shows provide a strong platform to conduct business, create new connections and deliver more visibility to any company. The truth is, many exhibitors are unable to capitalize on these opportunities. Why is it that some exhibitors like Mr. Brown hit a home run and many others leave feeling that they were benched?

Mr. Brown has exhibited at several hundred trade shows over time. Those trade shows exposed him to the marketplace across America and helped him grow his business.

The next few chapters will show how small, simple, basic, creative, no brainer steps can differentiate you from your competition.

Anyone can spend money and get recognized. But getting recognized, attracting new clients and growing business without spending an arm and a leg is a stroke of genius

And the following seven chapters are proof of that.

CHAPTER

CHANCE PE DANCE

Do you believe in sharing?

CHANCE PE DANCE

"You have infinite potential,
take your first step forward." – Mr. Brown

The first time Kow introduced me to Mr. Brown, I was in awe of his character. Here was a man who had met his dreams face to face, who made strong choices every day and stuck to them without ever taking his eyes off the prize. Mr. Brown is the definition of the phrase *chance pe dance* (an opportunist who is always twisting, turning and dancing to the tune of every opportunity presented to him).

Before meeting Mr. Brown, I had never heard of the concept of *chance pe dance*. He used a story of a lucky coin to explain it to me and continued with a few more tales that exemplified this same concept. But they weren't just stories you see; they were true-life experiences from which anyone could learn. It turns out that he had used the concept of *chance pe dance* throughout his career to capitalize on every chance he got to provide excellent customer service. He explained that if you do not take the first step and act on chance, then that opportunity will be lost, and nothing will happen. With this story I realized right then and there that I needed this man as a mentor, so I shall share this story of a coin with you first.

Reno, Nevada - Summer Show

A trip to Nevada was where, for the first time, Mr. Brown and his firm were given permission to present their merchandise for that specific buying group. He was moving up the industry ladder and there was a lot of pressure to succeed, but the odds were stacked against him and his sales team in Reno. Being new to that buying group, as well as the trade show scene, he had no idea where to start or what to expect. He had no client meetings set up either. The only luck he had going in his favor was that his entire team was charged up. The team had made elaborately detailed preparations for the event and they were ready to rally. No precious stone would go left unturned or unsold!

To clear a mind that is often clogged with New York City stress, Mr. Brown usually preferred to flip through a travel book and travel the host city, town, or even state for a couple of days before a trade show starts. After that detox, all negative thoughts were cleared, and he was ready to face any trade show challenge.

Before that convention, Mr. Brown found time to drive through a beautiful desert full of vast open space and fresh dry air to Virginia City. It was there, in the mid-1800s, that the first major silver deposit was discovered in the United States and everything around the town had boomed afterwards: a good omen for success at the trade show. He passed through several small towns, drove up a hill and finally arrived in the historic downtown, which felt like entering an old western movie set.

After breakfast Mr. Brown was eager to see what the town had to offer. He stepped through a casino door and could just imagine the hustle and bustle of the olden days when silver was pumping through the city's veins. He was pleased to see that not much of its' historical interior had changed. They had even kept the original slot machines, complete with their original operating levers, as well as old framed photos hanging on the wall.

Since it was early morning, not many patrons were on the casino floor, so he strolled past the bright lights and jingles of machines to find an associate. Before he could ask someone if one of the old pictures was available to purchase, his sneaker hit a small token. Suddenly, the token started to roll ahead of him with a musical ring. He followed the sound, watching the token until it finally came to a stop. It was a beautiful shimmering coin. He picked it up and couldn't tell if it was an old dollar coin or some sort of poker chip. He went to the dealer on the floor and asked if he could keep it. The dealer informed him that this was just a souvenir coin from the casino and of course he could keep it. Mr. Brown forgot all about the photos, enamored instead with the coin. Soon, it was time to end his sightseeing tour and return to the trade show to make some real money.

Back in Reno, the five days of the show flew by quickly as he and his sales team presented merchandise and spoke to prospective clients. The hard work that had gone into their initial preparation was rewarded handsomely during the first few days of the convention and everyone on his team was satisfied with the results. Before they knew it, it was Wednesday, the last day of the trade show. As soon as the doors opened at 10 a.m. their booth was flooded with clients. It was almost closing time, but as per their policy, they stayed open late to wait for one last potential client, even though it had already been a successful week.

Mr. Brown could feel relief in the air from all the exhibitors around him who, after five to six days, were ready to pack up and go home. Some of them had even turned off their display lights so they could cool off well before closing time. Other sellers were pulling heavy duty tape across cardboard boxes filled with leftover items. Amid everyone winding down, Mr. Brown noticed a young couple walking leisurely through the aisle with their children walking slowly behind them. The couple seemed pleased with their purchases and didn't pay much attention to Mr. Brown or his team members as they passed their booth. They were heading straight to the exit, having finished for the day.

Mr. Brown put his hand in his pockets as he kept an eye out for one more client and realized that he still had the souvenir coin from the beginning of his trip. It had already brought him plenty of luck at the trade show. He pulled the coin from his pocket and gave it to the little boy as he walked by. "This souvenir is for you, young man," Mr. Brown said. The boy and his sister looked at the shiny coin the same way Mr. Brown had marveled at it earlier, totally surprised by the gesture. Both children ran excitedly to their parents who were almost out of the buying hall. Mr. Brown stood there, amused by the equally surprised reaction on the parents' faces after the little boy handed his dad the coin to inspect. A moment later, the entire family returned to his booth.

"Hey there, my friend. My name is Mr. Pearl and we are visiting from Freeport, Illinois," the man said, reaching out a hand. He went on to introduce his wife and children. "Thank you very much for this lovely souvenir you gave my son. It was very nice of you. I know it's closing time but what do you guys supply?"

Mr. Brown, always open for business, smiled and said, "Well sir, please don't worry about the time." He went on to explain what he manufactured and supplied nationwide.

"Wow," Mr. Pearl said, "I am looking for a supplier who can cater to all these items under one roof."

Mr. Brown said, "Sir, please consider us for your needs. We are new exhibitors, and this is our very first convention in this buying group." As always, his team was behind him, ready to jump into action. "Can I see some of your products? If I like them, I will place a small order," Mr. Pearl said.

Mr. Brown invited his family to sit and make themselves comfortable before he started presenting samples. While Mr. Brown presented various selections for over half an hour after closing hours, the children were content to play with the coin in the aisle. Mr. Pearl made pages of notes for future reference and consulted with his wife to make decisions. By the time he finished ordering, the sale was close to $25,000. Who would have thought a new business relationship could blossom from the gift of a souvenir coin? Should we call this a stroke of luck or good karma? Either way, it proves that when hard work and opportunity collide, the result is always fruitful.

It didn't take long for Mr. Brown to build strong ties with Mr. Pearl, who is still a loyal client to this day. Both his children have grown and are learning various parts of his business. His son is now taller than he is and would someday like to take over the business. As of wrapping this story, Mr. Brown has generated sales of over $750,000 with Mr. Pearl. Not bad considering it all started with something given selflessly with no intention of getting anything in return.

THE WRAP UPS – BY MR. BROWN

- *Use every resource at your disposal to give and give and give.*
- *Lady Luck comes in many forms; a coin is just one of them.*
- *Act generously whenever you can, returns will multiply.*

CHAPTER

5

FIFTEEN MINUTES TO $5,000

Have you ever challenged yourself?

FIFTEEN MINUTES TO $5,000

"First in. Last out." – Mr. Brown

How many of you watch sports? How many of you play sports? It can be basketball, baseball, football, cricket or even skiing etc. Have you ever seen an athlete give up and forfeit with half an hour left in the game? The answer is no. Those few last moments can change the entire outcome of the game. Similarly, do not think of business as mere work, think of it as a sport. Go all out and even harder in the last minutes of closing a store, trade show, exhibition, convention or anywhere there is an interaction between a buyer and seller. Why? You never know who will cross your path to extend a handshake to. As we saw in "Chance Pe Dance," the last prospective client of the day can be a game changer.

Mr. Brown is always disappointed when he observes salespeople, even CEOs and owners, begin to pack up for the day before the closing time. He fails to understand the reason for this kind of behavior. The purpose of every firm that would *spend money* to go to trade shows, or on advertising, or on incentives, etc., is to service existing clients, meet prospective clients, build up a substantial client base and take as many orders as possible. All these factors add up to the bottom line: you are there *to sell*. So why not take as many orders as you possibly can to make a profit?

Let me use an everyday example we will call Store #1: Would you make a purchase in a store where the salespeople are just hanging around talking to each other or working to close the store rather than acknowledging your presence? I guarantee you won't, unless you're desperate for something. Your first impression on entering such a store will be that these guys don't care about their job or about helping you find what you need. Even if someone does help you, you might feel like you're bothering them. To make matters worse, they won't exhibit genuine enthusiasm as they present you with a product, since all they want to do is pack up. You will probably leave the store or showroom unsatisfied and without any purchases.

Now let's say it is closing time nearby at Store #2 which is Store #1's competition. Every salesperson is on the floor actively arranging merchandise and putting things back into their proper place. Someone steps away from her work to greet you. With a lovely smile she asks, "How may I help you this evening?" I bet with that small gesture she has already won half the battle of earning your purchase. She presents various selections of merchandise and you forget that it's almost past closing time. You look up at the person taking care of you, but she doesn't reveal a single hint of annoyance or glance at her watch. Even if you don't make a purchase that night, you know that you are welcome back any time.

Store #1 will complain that business is slow. They have the mindset that there are not enough customers. Store #2 sees the potential of everyone that walks through the door and it gets reflected in their sales numbers. One has mastered the art of customer care while the other has fallen far from the mark. These differences in service occur in every industry. It is the level of service that differentiates a successful business from a failed one.

Here are some more of Mr. Brown's experiences where those last few minutes made all the difference.

Columbus, Ohio - Fall Trade Show

Let's begin with Ida and Ivy. It was a Saturday in Columbus; Ohio and the trade show was closing at 6 p.m. It happened to be 5:30 p.m. when Mr. Brown noticed the usual ordeal.

Vendors were beginning to close and pack up for the day. Mr. Brown's booth was still open, and his sales team was joking around with each other when a neighboring vendor, a pearl dealer, came up to him and asked why they weren't closing yet. Mr. Brown explained that they were waiting for that one last customer who would soon come and buy.

His neighbor said, "Oh, I see, you are waiting for your appointment."

Mr. Brown clarified, "No, I am waiting for the one last customer I have never met before. There is somebody somewhere and I will close a sale with them before I close for the day."

The neighbor laughed and left saying, "You guys are crazy, good night."

Sure enough, at 6 p.m. on the dot, two ladies were looking around the trade show with a shopping list full of items they still needed to buy. It seemed as if they had arrived late. The sight of Mr. Brown's still-open booth caught the eye of the younger lady as she moved down the aisle. She slowed down to look at his selection more closely. Knowing he only had about thirty seconds to grab her attention, Mr. Brown greeted both ladies without hesitation and pulled out a pair of 2 carat total weight diamond earrings from inside his display case. The older lady continued to walk and did not stop at the booth.

The younger lady was strictly business as she asked him shortly, "How much?"

He replied, "Only $5,000 dollars."

He could sense that she liked the price for the deal that

was offered to her. "I'm sorry, we have an appointment and we're already running late," the younger lady explained.

"I understand," he said. "But ma'am, here is my card. I am still open. Please allow me to show you our products after you have finished with your appointment."

She hurried to catch up with her boss. Mr. Brown's team realized they had no idea how long the appointment would last. Waiting could have been all for nothing. They did not even know if the ladies would come back. But still, they waited.

With no one else around it felt as if they had been waiting for over an hour. Finally, when the ladies returned, they used their last bits of energy to offer genuine smiles to them. The team jumped up to help Mr. Brown. He was looking forward to cementing this deal and proving to his tired team members that it was always worth it to stay open late.

The younger lady, who introduced herself as Ida, explained how she and her boss Ivy were stuck in traffic on their way in from Canton, Ohio. They were upset that they had missed most of the show for that day but were pleased to look at Mr. Brown's merchandise. Ivy told him, "I am glad you stopped Ida. I like your product and I will purchase it but be sure to send me this same exact piece. These earrings are the ones I want." Their purchase ended up being the original $5,000: a small beginning but an excellent sale since it was the hard-earned result of patience.

The next morning, the very first question Mr. Brown's neighbor asked was, "So did that one last customer come?" Mr. Brown could hear the sarcasm in his tone. He smiled and told him that sure enough, that last customer had come through after all.

By the time the holiday season ended around January 15th of that year, they touched around $100,000 in sales with Ida and Ivy from Ohio. What an excellent growth in the business! One day, Ida called and told Mr. Brown that Ivy wanted to run a retirement sale and they needed help in supplying merchandise. Mr. Brown was delighted that staying open for an extra fifteen minutes after closing one day could bring in so much business.

Smyrna, Georgia - Fall Trade Show

It was the last day of a trade show in Smyrna, Georgia and getting near closing time with many booths pulling merchandise from their displays. As usual, Mr. Brown stuck to his guns. He often reminded his fellow exhibitors how much time was left and that there were still buyers perusing the rows. He wanted to see his fellow exhibitors succeed as well, but few others possessed his drive and patience. The fact that they were willing to give up and go gave his team more motivation to stay open late, so much so that they decided to play a game. They challenged themselves to generate an extra $5,000 in sales before calling it quits for the day. They scanned the hall looking for any potential client walking towards the exit.

Soon they spotted a gentleman coming toward them. The team quickly discussed what it would take to grab his attention. Mr. Brown stepped up and said, "Sir, I am short $5,000 in sales towards my closing target. What can you do? Can you help me?" This was not a normal question. As he suspected, the man laughed. In fact, he laughed at Mr. Brown as if he had never heard this kind of statement from anyone in his whole life. He introduced himself, clearly amused, as Earle from Alabama. "Show me what you got," he said, entertained. Right on cue, the team stepped in to help present their merchandise and pull out Earle's selections.

Earle said, "Keep adding my selections and stop at $5,000, would you? Give me some time to pay. I don't need merchandise until early November. The order is going to be for the holiday season." Earle even pulled out his trade references to prove that his word was honorable. He also told Mr. Brown that he could speak to one of his trade suppliers who happened to be packing up a couple booths down. The exhibitor just happened to be a friend of Mr. Brown's! After checking in with Jerry, who said that trusting Earle's word was as good as depositing money in the bank, Mr. Brown agreed to the deal. Though it was one of his rules never to give merchandise without payment first, Mr. Brown let Earle take his merchandise with him, only because he trusted Jerry's word. And Earle had been a good sport and helped Mr. Brown win the game against his team!

The team members were good sports and felt equally satisfied with the successful final sale of the show. Though it wasn't a huge amount, it was an excellent foundation with a solid client and had been a fun game to play. Now they could happily pack up shop and head home to rest.

Success with Earle from Alabama followed as well. Over time, Earle became a great friend, in addition to an honorable and honest client. He loved pizza and before he left the show during their first meeting, he told Mr. Brown that if he wanted him to come and buy from him next time, then Mr. Brown must save him a slice of pizza. For the next few years he was always the last client on the last day of the show in Smyrna. The team kept their end of the bargain as well and made sure Earle got that slice of pizza he'd requested.

After a few years he started to come with his daughter and Mr. Brown saw that he had lost a lot of weight. It turned out that Earle had undergone bypass surgery. His daughter strictly said no more pizza for her dad, only fruits and veggies. So next time he came, Mr. Brown offered fruits and veggies. Over time, Earle must have purchased over $250,000 worth of goods as he munched on those slices of pizza, apples and carrots.

It's not always that first sale with a client that matters. In both Columbus and Smyrna, the purchases were $5,000, which was a great start. However, even if a purchase was $5, it would have been just as important. One should always think of the future to come with a client and the potential for growth together.

Now do you see why it is so important to always act open until the very end of a show. If you make someone feel welcome, even if they cannot purchase at that time, they will most likely return later. This is just one of the ways Mr. Brown keeps his clients coming back for more. He would never make a client feel as if they were bothering him. A sale is always worth waiting for.

THE WRAP UPS – BY MR. BROWN

- *The last fifteen minutes before closing can be a revenue changer.*
- *Smile even when you've run out of energy.*
- *To grow any business, you must have an insatiable appetite.*
- *No sale is too small. Give each person your undivided attention as if they were a million-dollar client.*

CHAPTER 6

VIP

Do you wash your hands before extending for a handshake?

VIP

"Pissing brings relief, so does profit." – Mr. Brown

Do you ever think about doing business where you do your business? This (VIP) Very Important Piss is just one example of how the letter P can stand for many important tools in business. It stands for profit, patience, persistence, possibilities or even piss. Yes, piss. Did you know that this basic human function can lead to striking up a conversation with anybody? Whether you're in line for the men's room or lady's room or even in a neighboring stall (pass the toilet paper, please!). Mr. Brown taught me that even this room is a conference room that few take advantage of. It's a surprisingly ideal place to foster a business relationship if you let it, because there is no distraction or disturbance.

Typically, when you first meet someone, your greeting starts with a simple handshake. At tradeshows and conventions, half the battle is getting someone to shake your hand. Many people pretend they don't see you. Sometimes they walk the other way. Other times they do anything to avoid eye contact. But if you put your hand right out there in front of them, it's hard for them not to meet you halfway. A lot of vendors are afraid to initiate this first contact. They are afraid of being misperceived, misrepresented or worried about saying something that ends up having a negative effect.

Mr. Brown and Kow were never afraid of this. By his fourth year with the company Kow had already learned a great deal from Mr. Brown and he knew that whenever you want to make an introduction, you just need to extend your hand. And, just like that, half of the battle is won. There's a quote from the movie *We Bought a Zoo* that stuck in Mr. Brown's head: "Sometimes all you need is twenty seconds of insane courage." Trying to make an introduction doesn't exactly require an insane amount of courage, but it does require bravery because whenever you put yourself out there, there's always the chance of rejection.

Covington, Kentucky - Kentucky Convention Center - Summer

Kow headed to a cocktail party at the convention. It was around 7:00 p.m. and everyone there was in the best of moods after a few drinks. Kow, along with Mr. Brown, began to mingle with new friends, making connections that would lay a firm foundation for a new business relationship.

After a few bottles of beer their kidneys were working hard. They both lasted until late in the evening before heading to the men's room for a little relief. As Kow and Mr. Brown began to relieve themselves, a middle-aged, casually dressed man walked up to the urinal right in between them. It caught them a bit off guard that he chose that urinal, but he seemed more than a little drunk and probably needed some major bladder relief. Both of his hands were occupied, one with a bottle of beer and the other with a glass of scotch. He placed them on top of the urinal so he could lean on the wall for support. As he began to do his business, a song erupted from his lungs and he sang aloud with his eyes closed.

Amused, Mr. Brown decided to engage him in conversation by saying, "Hey, how's it going?" The man opened his eyes and briefly smiled before going back to pissing and singing. Now Mr. Brown was very curious about this interesting character. "Who are you?" Only members of the convention party were in that part of the building and they were all there to mingle so why not mingle even if the mingling happened at a urinal?

The man must have had a lot of drinks because the piss was still flowing as he replied, "Billy is my name, who are you folks?"

"We're vendors and it's our first time here at the Kentucky Convention Center," Mr. Brown explained.

The mysterious gentleman finished his business and turned to Mr. Brown. "I'm a retailer from Mitchell, South Dakota. I'll come see you tomorrow."

Kow and Mr. Brown had heard this line from many other retailers whom they never saw again. Not wanting to let Billy off the hook that easily, Kow decided to dance at this chance and jumped into the conversation saying, "Please allow me to write your name and cell number on the back of my nametag and I'll write my information on your nametag so we don't forget to see each other tomorrow. With your permission, I'll call you tomorrow morning to remind you to visit us at the convention."

Billy grabbed his drink and said, "Okay guys, I will see you tomorrow! But, before I leave, give me one person who will vouch for you."

This request came as a bit of a shock and Mr. Brown wondered if someone had set him up. Billy seemed genuinely interested, albeit cautious. After just a few minutes of conversation at a urinal he was ready to do business. Was there a hidden camera somewhere? Was this a joke or had their seconds of insane courage really worked?

Mr. Brown and Kow looked at each other trying to figure out how to convince Billy that they were excellent suppliers. To win his confidence, they had to find someone near the men's room and have that person vouch for them on the spot before Billy headed back to the party and potentially brushed off the encounter. As we have learned, luck comes in many forms, sometimes a coin, but many times in the shape of a human. They turned around to find someone and here was Mr. Burket from Texarkana, Texas, father of Mr. Brown's dear friend and retailer, Tara. He just happened to be walking towards them, probably on the way to use the very same men's room.

"Mr. Burket," Mr. Brown said, "This gentleman here wants to know about our firm and about the level of service we provide."

Mr. Burket spoke quickly, clearly in a hurry to use the men's room, saying, "Sir, don't look any further. These are the best people to work with. My daughter has been buying almost every jewelry product that they offer for over the last ten years. You will not be disappointed. I guarantee you. Now please excuse me."

Kow had no idea what to say as Mr. Burket entered the men's room and Billy headed back to the party. Moments earlier, he hadn't really believed they'd hook Billy as a client; how could anyone expect someone else to vouch for them right when they needed it, especially near the men's room? But something told him that Billy would show up the next day without a reminder.

Sure enough, a well-groomed man showed up at their booth the next day at 10:00 a.m. asking for Kow. Billy looked very businesslike, his two hands now occupied with a notepad and pen. What a change from last night! He didn't seem to be suffering from a hangover of any kind as he spent two hours looking at their merchandise before placing an order.

As he was leaving, he invited them to visit him at his place in South Dakota for that coming year's fall and holiday season purchases. Before leaving, he said, "Do not underestimate the power of pissing." They all cracked up.

About three months after that night at the convention center, Kow was travelling to South Dakota to visit a few clients. After the visit, he went to a little cafe in Sioux Falls. As he was eating, he remembered Billy and pulled up the road map. It turned out he was only 90 miles from the town of Mitchell which Billy had invited him to visit. Kow wondered if Billy would even remember him. He knew it was a long shot, but what the heck! After all, Kow was so used to hearing, "No thank you," that it wouldn't faze him if he heard those words again. He decided to go ahead and call Billy, who did in fact remember him right away and was thrilled to hear that he was in South Dakota. He invited Kow to meet him the next day.

As it turned out, the Billy who was waiting at the entrance of his store to welcome Kow was a conservative Christian. His wife did not like for him to drink. In her presence Kow didn't mention specifically just how he'd first encountered Billy, which earned him more respect and trust. Billy quickly became Kow's good friend and an excellent client. His second order was around $20,000. Shortly after, Billy became a $100,000 customer.

Had Kow and Mr. Brown not said anything that night in the men's room, Billy would probably never have become a client, or even a friend. What does this go to show? You do not need a big conference room, sales office or fancy showroom to do business. Clearly, there's never a bad time or place to strike up a conversation.

THE WRAP UPS – BY MR. BROWN

- *Always take someone up on their offer to visit.*
- *Do not be intimidated by the opportunity that exists in the least expected places.*
- *You don't have to know a person to strike up a conversation.*

CHAPTER

7

IFS AND BUTTS

Do you sit on your butt?

IFS AND BUTTS

"Anyone in range is a potential new client." – Mr. Brown

Sitting in a chair, making yourself comfortable and answering questions from your seat is a classic case of the Comfort Zone. You cannot expect a sale to land in your lap. This is just wishful thinking. Whom would you consider working with? A person speaking with you while sitting in a chair or a person who comes forward and shakes your hand ready to answer your questions? Who is more professional? Let's try to find the answer from one of Mr. Brown's encounters in Las Vegas.

Las Vegas, Nevada - Sands Convention Center

Everything was glittering at the summer show in Vegas. So much so that clients were flowing over like champagne. The trade show was a five-day event, starting Friday and ending Tuesday. Five days of a trade show can become monotonous for some, but not for Mr. Brown's team. It was their second year in the show, and even though they only had a small booth location, the team members felt proud of it and worked very hard. They displayed their merchandise inside the showcase and on the table inside the booth near the sidewall. Basically, they were trying to catch the attention of anyone passing by.

On Monday afternoon, the day before the show's closing, clients were still flowing over. Mr. Brown was working in the booth with a client and everyone else on his team was occupied. Out of the corner of his eye he saw a couple walking down the aisle. The young lady had a shopping list in hand. As she approached, something caught her attention inside his booth. The couple took a step forward for a closer look at the merchandise. Judging from her expression, Mr. Brown realized that she wanted information. He asked the client he was working with if he would excuse him for a moment while he stood up to greet the couple. He then pulled out a few diamond bracelets from the table and gave them to her to examine. She passed them to her husband, and they spoke about the excellent quality, but her expression turned serious when she learned the price. They returned to the middle of the aisle with the bracelets now on her wrist as they discussed. Mr. Brown heard her hushed words, "Honey, we've been paying a lot more for these items and these are very well made."

Mr. Brown did not want the client who was waiting to feel that he had forgotten about him so he reassured him that he would be back in two minutes. When the couple returned, the lady asked if she could buy the samples, which was precisely what he'd been hoping to hear. In fact, judging by her enthusiastic tone he hoped those folks would be added to his growing roster of clients. At this point, his experience had made him good at analyzing and assessing a buyer's intentions after only a brief meeting. The couple's approach and positive attitude convinced him that they had the potential to turn out to be valuable clients.

When they asked him if they could buy and take the merchandise with them his answer of course was no. The lady was shocked. Neither wife nor husband expected this answer, as they were well-rated and respected in their local, social, and business communities. He calmly explained his business rules and apologized for being unprofessional, as he had neither a seat to offer them nor enough time now to present other merchandise. Mr. Brown did not want to miss the dance that this golden chance presented. He wanted to sell more than only that which they had seen. He assured them that he would do his best to earn their business if they wouldn't mind setting up an appointment the next morning to see his whole line of merchandise. When they said they were leaving that day he went into customer service overdrive: "I will make special arrangements to meet both of you and pick you up at the entrance at 8:30 a.m. sharp." He planned to ask the show management office for special permission to escort them to his booth early, even though the show didn't open until 10:00 a.m.

Mr. Brown gave them no reason to refuse, so they happily agreed, introducing themselves as Al and Mary from Leesburg, Virginia. They recognized the fact that he was going above and beyond to take care of them. Sure enough, the next morning, Al and Mary arrived at the door sharply at 8:25 a.m. He couldn't believe his eyes when they approached; they were holding large cups of coffee and about a dozen muffins for the members of his team. The couple understood that starting early at 8:30 a.m. meant the team would be having a very long day. They said this was the least they could do for meeting them before they headed back to the D.C. area.

The morning proved to be the perfect time to show the couple merchandise without any distractions or disturbance. Since there was hardly anyone around that early, Mary and Al took their time browsing the entire line. They ended up placing their first order for around $25,000. How's that for the first sale of the day!

Before leaving, Mr. Brown thanked them from the bottom of his heart for coming early to view the line and for being so thoughtful. Before leaving, Mary said that from the next year forward, they would like to be the very first clients, in the first hour of the first day, to enter his booth. How could he refuse such a genuine request?

To this day, he has kept his promise. Mary and Al always arrive on time as the first clients on the first day of the show, sharply at 10:00 a.m. Mr. Brown believes that every show or conference must begin with the right people whose initial doses of positive energy set the tone for the rest of the show. And it doesn't hurt to start with a strong dose of coffee either!

Before a trade show ends, Mr. Brown's friend Neil always comes over and asks how the last day went. When Mr. Brown told him about Al and Mary, Neil couldn't believe what had happened. He'd been trying to break in with the two of them for over eight years since they were AAA+ rated and loyal clients. "You did the right thing by setting an early appointment," he said, with a bit of envy. In Las Vegas, sometimes you get lucky and sometimes you don't. Mr. Brown made his own luck by taking the initiative to talk to Al and Mary. Neil was right, he sure did hit the jackpot meeting them, they quickly became million-dollar clients. Does this work?

After a few years, the couple brought one of their daughters to the show. Mr. Brown could sense that in due time, the next generation would enter the business. As Al and Mary's children began to make most of the buying decisions, Mr. Brown maintained his side of the bargain and continued to suggest his best deals and selections. Through their mutual respect (and mutual love for muffins and coffee), they weren't just his clients anymore. Now, they were part of his family.

THE WRAP UPS – BY MR. BROWN

- *Even a small boat can summon a whale.*
- *Always have a big appetite when selling to the right customer.*
- *Do not sit around waiting for a sale; get off your butt and make it happen.*
- *Always start your day with a positive client, you will line up your day for success.*

RULES ARE MADE FOR SOME REASON

Do you like to break the rules?

RULES ARE MADE FOR SOME REASON

"Want to lose a customer? Use the word NO." – Mr. Brown

Exhibiting at a trade show is not cheap. With a long list of expenses like travel cost, advertising and exhibition costs in the back of your mind, it's important to optimize the return during these shows. Sometimes, this makes vendors act reckless. The goal is to talk to absolutely anyone and everyone. Keep in mind that even though most people who go to shows are honest, there are a few just looking to make a quick buck. The same can be said for any industry. If you don't nail down a specific set of rules to protect your business, you might get taken advantage of in the heat of a moment.

Las Vegas, Nevada - September

In Las Vegas Mr. Brown's team had created something special: a handwritten neon poster board sign. This sign was not professional by any means, but it did the job of listing the special deals they were offering at the show. Mr. Brown prefers to save money and never spend frivolously, so it made more sense to spend a few bucks on quality poster-board and make the sign themselves rather than pay someone to make it for them, especially since the sign would only be used once at this particular show. It was an inexpensive, creative solution, but would it catch some attention? It certainly set them apart from the crowd and stood out as a bright eye sore.

Mr. Brown was in his booth, ready for a prospective customer, when a couple passing through the aisle stopped. The young lady, Heather from St. George, Utah, inquired about the merchandise as listed on the charming sign.

She decided to purchase a few items and quickly wrote him a check for $135. She wanted to take the items she had selected back home with her, but as per Mr. Brown's business policy, he explained that the goods would be shipped from New York as soon as her check had cleared. She started to turn red and he watched as her temper rose. "I have never bounced a check in my life!" she exclaimed. "This check is good!"

His answer was simple: "I believe and trust you, but I have to follow certain guidelines with a first-time buyer. Please put yourself in my shoes. It is not meant as an offense to you ma'am."

Here was a buyer with whom he had no prior history, a situation that if not handled carefully, could easily lead to the loss of a wonderful prospective client. Your experience and expertise can only produce a desired result if you try to satisfy both sides of the deal. So, he went on to explain his policy and offered to even fax her copies of bad checks that he had been given in the past. He assured her that when her check was cleared, he would ship the goods to her immediately. In the future, once the account was established, she could take anything she wanted right there on the spot. Her eyes started to tear up. He was feeling sorry for her because she was clearly offended. She gave her check to Mr. Brown and then left the booth with her husband.

After the show ended the next day Mr. Brown returned to his New York office. The first thing he noticed on his desk was a long fax. In those days, they were still using thermal paper, so all that extra paper made the fax seem even longer. He went straight to the bottom of the page to see who had the free time to write such a fax and was shocked to read the name of the owner of the company. It was none other than Heather from the Las Vegas convention show to whom Mr. Brown had refused to give merchandise. She wrote that she was upset with the salesperson who had attended to her at the convention, claiming that he had refused to give her the merchandise by not accepting her check. She also mentioned that she had never bounced a check in her life. Basically, she was repeating the same arguments she had given him in person, though now her anger was even more potent.

Mr. Brown called Heather immediately to apologize for the way she felt about his actions at the show. He explained that he was the very person she was complaining about and that he was ready for any punishment that she considered fit for his behavior. Mr. Brown went on to explain that this business was his baby and that a $135 check may seem like peanuts, but there were certain basic rules that he had to lay down for his business to succeed and run smoothly. If he had accepted her check as if it were cash, he would be breaking the rules of his policy. He apologized again and hung up.

After their conversation, it finally clicked with Heather that his policy had nothing to do with her personally and he did not sell merchandise simply for the sake of profit. He was genuine in that he wanted a long-term business relationship and not just a short-term gain. Over time, her confidence in doing business with him multiplied. She started to recommend Mr. Brown to various trade groups as well as her business friends. In fact, her confidence in his business values grew so high that she would bring people with her to his showroom. He generated over $150,000 with Heather during that short period of time. They still laugh about her reaction to his initial refusal of that first $135 check. The only faxes he gets from her now are orders for more merchandise.

Columbus, Ohio - Summer Show - August

This next story that took place at a weekend conference in Ohio, ended up being just as dramatic. It was a Sunday at a summer show that was ending at 4:00 p.m. It must have been around an hour before when Mr. Brown saw an entire team, led by a tough looking man, coming towards his showroom booth. It seemed they were on route to the exit however, Mr. Brown's corner booth caught one of the ladies' attention. Her eyes went straight to the princess cut diamond earrings displayed inside the showcase. She asked him to pull out one display so she could view it more closely. Soon her entire team was at the booth looking over her shoulder.

She turned and started discussing the products on display with the tough-looking man in his sixties who was her boss Doug, from Westlake, Ohio. He looked at the merchandise and offered to buy the entire display right then and there, explaining that he wanted to carry it all with him. Mr. Brown politely told him that the products would be promptly shipped from his office after he returned to New York. Like Heather before him, Doug became upset and annoyed. He simply couldn't understand the logic behind the refusal. Here he was, willing to buy and pay for a whole display in person. Mr. Brown could literally feel the force of the man's frustration. He could tell that Doug was running a successful, possibly multi-million-dollar business back in Ohio with this attitude and sizeable team behind him, but he still did not budge on his policy.

In the end, Doug got so fed up with Mr. Brown's various ways of rephrasing the same answer that he said, "So what do you want from me then? Here, here is my wife. Keep her but give me the merchandise I want." Mr. Brown knew this was a joke, but the man was trying so hard to get him to back down that he had to physically take a few steps back.

Politely, he replied, "Sir your wife is precious and priceless. Nobody can put a price tag on her." Doug appreciated that answer and so did his wife. Mr. Brown could see him starting to cool down as he continued, "Please, put yourself in my shoes. Allow me to ship to you from my office. I will not even charge for shipping. Do not take this policy of ours as an offense to you." Doug finally gave in and handed over his check, his ego taking a bruising.

Before leaving he told him, "Kid, you are more stubborn than me. I am disappointed for not getting to walk out with my goodies. But I am happy that in today's day and age, someone is following rules and policies. Someday you should come to my showroom and tell my entire sales team the reason for your refusal to give me what I wanted. I don't have time to hear it all now."

When Mr. Brown made it to Ohio again, he did not go empty handed. He brought ice cream for Doug and his entire team. They all had a laugh over the fact that Doug had offered his wife as payment. They became friends on the spot, over a laugh and a handshake.

Years later, Mr. Brown received a letter addressed to him, which turned out to be from Doug. Since America was in a great recession, Doug's business was feeling its effects. The purpose of his letter was to let Mr. Brown know that his holiday business had been poor and that he needed more time to pay his bills. He went on to admit that he had missed a lot of sales from the lower price point items that Mr. Brown had suggested and was feeling sorry for not listening to him.

During my own life I have come across few people who would write me a letter about how I'd been right and how they should have listened to me. It was the same for Mr. Brown, who immediately called Doug and thanked him for taking the time to write. Without batting an eye, he told Doug that after such a strong business relationship, of course he could take some more time to pay. He went on to say that he was sorry things didn't go well. He continued, "My doors are always and will always be open for you. If I can do anything for you, please do not hesitate to ask." After that incident their mutual respect increased tenfold. They have continued to work with each other to this day with nothing but increased sales after that hiccup.

Warning:

It is a shame when hard working traders and exhibitors drive or fly to show venues, set up booths hoping to make successful sales, and get screwed over the course of a just few days. They come puppy-eyed, hoping to build future business relationships with clients and end up stumbling over proper protocol. Before you know it, rules are not followed and mistakes are made. Many times, greed supersedes all norms and they stop thinking with common sense. Goods are delivered against payment of checks, especially on the last day of a show. People are happy about a successful show and let their guards down. A couple of days later, a surprise arrives in the mail with a check returned because of insufficient funds.

Who is responsible for this loss? Not the sucker who extracted the goods and wrote the bad check, but the trader supplier who accepted it against their better judgment. The bottom line is that once you set the rules you must stick to them even if you must sacrifice some sales. If the person on the other side of the table is truly a businessman or woman, they will understand that you must carry out the policies you have designed to protect your business and they will eventually respect you for it.

Take it from Mr. Brown, against Sam I Am's strong objection, one of his sales team members lowered his defenses and gave in to delivering merchandise without first cashing the check, losing $34,000. He made the rules, laid down policies and then broke them. While he accepted full responsibility for that early blow to the business, a single mistake was enough for him to stand by the fact that rules are made for many reasons.

THE WRAP UPS – BY MR. BROWN

- *Rules are the seat belt in business.*
- *Show your clients that you are hungry for their business, but not greedy.*
- *"Put yourself in my shoes" is the best way to help a customer understand your side of the story.*
- *Always keep a cool head. Do not get intimidated by an angry customer or someone more successful than you.*

MS. OPPORTUNITY OR MR. BLEW IT

Why do you exhibit at the trade show?

MS. OPPORTUNITY OR MR. BLEW IT

"No one is going to walk up and hand you a sale." – Mr. Brown

---

It is probably no surprise that people would love to get paid without having to work for it. A salesperson with no motivation might be eager to label someone as a missed opportunity instead of a potential opportunity. A sales team without proper homework fails to recognize a big fish when they see one. Debbie from Jackson, Tennessee, one of Mr. Brown's most trustworthy friends in the industry, told him a story that perfectly illustrates this point.

Las Vegas, Nevada - Summer Show

Now keep in mind, Debbie is old school. Her verbal commitment means as much as a written agreement drafted by a lawyer and signed by both parties. Well-respected in her town and local community, she is the epitome of a savvy businesswoman. As the CEO of a leading company, Debbie was in Las Vegas to attend a trade show. She arrived sharply at 10:00 a.m. on the first day with her associate who oversaw purchasing. They had an appointment to meet the salesperson who oversaw her sales district. She made the appointment to assure they would receive undivided attention with one on one interaction. Usually, when the trade show opens on the first day it is not busy unless someone happens to liquidate inventory. She started looking over various products in the showcases. All the salespeople were busy talking and eating breakfast.

Fifteen minutes had passed and still no one had approached her. Mind you, this booth was one of the largest at the show with plenty of salesmen and not a single person from the sales team, including the manager, took a step in her direction. She was no small fish! They just continued chatting amongst themselves as if she wasn't even there. Other suppliers were lining up and even desperate to earn her business, but here she was for her scheduled appointment and no one was bothering to greet her. Needless to say, she was extremely upset. She not only left the place immediately, but firmly decided against giving them any future business.

The salespeople and manager who failed that day are the same people who kept complaining that things were tough, business was slow, and nobody was buying. Since they were part of a big house and had many more opportunities to make money, they didn't even try. They simply expected the money to roll in without making much of an effort. The smallest effort goes a long way. If someone would have at least greeted her, this story would have had a much different ending.

Las Vegas, Nevada - Sands Expo

You can certainly find yourself in trouble if you don't make enough effort, but you can also find yourself in trouble when you make *too* much effort, which Mr. Brown learned at another trade show in Las Vegas. This show was a single day event, so if you failed to capitalize on every opportunity that came along, you would lose your chance until next year. In this kind of situation Mr. Brown never relaxes or sits down. He and his team go all out, stay focused, and work hard to optimize the biggest return. They spend money just to be there, so they make sure not to waste a second.

That day they greeted every single soul that passed by their booth trying to generate sales. Other exhibitors didn't have the same drive and preferred to speak with clients from their seats behind their displays until they showed clear signs of wanting to make a purchase. They were not salespeople but simply cashiers. Imagine to Mr. Brown's surprise, when in the midst of his hustle, a show coordinator named Audrie took him to the side and said, "I am sorry to tell you this, but there are a few exhibitors complaining that you guys are being aggressive so I have to request you to please tone it down."

Should he consider this a compliment or a criticism? Mr. Brown had no answer but politely said, "You and I both know we are here for a reason and that reason is business. Our business is not to sit on our butts."

He asked her to walk with him to the edge of the buying hall over by the entrance door. He pointed out a few vendors, "Look at most of the vendors at any show booth. Most of them are all perfectly relaxed, and look, some of the buyers are passing them by. Those guys don't even care. I have given clear instructions to my team members that unless they are going to fall flat on the ground from standing too long, they must stand and greet every single soul that passes through the aisle. They are just doing what I've asked of them: engaging people in conversation with a hello, good morning, or good afternoon. This is not aggressive; this is strictly a polite way to do business. We don't want to miss any opportunity that presents itself. I understand that it may come off as aggressive to some of these other vendors who do not want to get up and move, but my team sees every person here as an opportunity."

Our Mr. Brown was effective in conveying his message and

she agreed with his point, but before leaving requested that he tone it down just a bit. Mr. Brown went back to the booth and told his team what had happened. They were proud of what they saw as a compliment and felt even more charged up to sell.

In today's time and age many people want easy money. They think that people will just walk in and buy. They think it is not their job to guide them and educate them about the value of a product, even if they are getting paid for it. But the crazy part is, they still want to get paid and get their commission as if they are doing all the work.

The lesson here is plain and simple: if you don't care, trust me when I say that someone else will. In fact, that person is going to come in and take your client or your job. Do not be fooled into thinking you will get a second chance. Remember, you are living in the most competitive era in modern history. You had better care about your work, because in the end no one is going to give you money for free. You must view every opportunity as Ms. Opportunity and not become another Mr. Blew It.

THE WRAP UPS – BY MR. BROWN

- *If you don't care, someone else will.*
- *Do not wait for money to land in your lap. There is no such thing as free money.*
- *Create a culture of care as business grows.*
- *Greeting everyone isn't aggressive, it is simply a way of doing business.*

CHAPTER

THE MOST EXPENSIVE BREAKFAST I EVER HAD

Are you persistent with patience?

THE MOST EXPENSIVE BREAKFAST I EVER HAD

"Have you ever surprised anyone?" – Mr. Brown

As I said before, the goal of exhibiting in any trade show is to optimize the return on investment. An easy concept to comprehend. The more eggs in your basket the better the omelet. Each trade show is a source of unlimited opportunities and Mr. Brown always treated them as if his next big client was playing hide and seek with him in the aisles. He would do all that he could to find him or her, which would usually pay him off in the long run.

The shows are the perfect platform for Mr. Brown to break the ice and lay a strong foundation for the future success of his business. But sometimes, he just couldn't find his next big client. Or worse, he found them but didn't get an opportunity to meet and click with them. As funny and as entertaining as Mr. Brown is, not everyone wants to do business with the eager young man the first time they meet.

Boston, Massachusetts - July

One such client, with whom Mr. Brown had always wanted to do business, was Jerry from Crestview, Florida. They were introduced briefly back in 2002. After that initial breaking of the ice Mr. Brown approached Jerry whenever he had the chance. Years went by and the man still wouldn't budge. Mr. Brown always expected to hear "I will keep you in mind" instead of a "yes." Jerry was set in his ways and did not need a new young supplier. Nevertheless, Mr. Brown was patient, following the age-old saying that patience and persistence will never let you down.

In March of 2004 his persistence finally paid off. As hopeful as the day they first met, Mr. Brown stopped to greet Jerry as he came walking down the aisle near his showroom. Jerry seemed like he was in a good mood so Mr. Brown took advantage of this opportunity and did all he could to keep his attention. Jerry looked over a few of Mr. Brown's products and to his shock, finally agreed to buy something from him.

"Okay, send me these only. I'll give them a try," he said with a smile. It was like music to our Mr. Brown's ears! He was not only happy that Jerry had stopped but he placed an order for $833. It was a footstep in the right direction and Mr. Brown felt proud of himself. He was looking forward to growing a business relationship with Jerry.

Unfortunately, to his utter disappointment, a year passed with hit and miss trades. He didn't make any progress with Jerry over the phone and he ended up back at square one with "I'll keep you in mind." He tried to stay positive reminding himself that at least he'd gained Jerry as a client for a short period of time.

A year later, in July of 2005, his team was in Boston at the Marriott Convention and Conference Center. At around 8:00 a.m. at the Marriott Hotel Restaurant, he was sipping coffee and eating breakfast with one of his young, energetic team members who went by the nickname of Sam I Am. Sam I Am had a big appetite, so for him, breakfast usually consisted of a couple of toasted cheese and vegetable sandwiches, hash browns and several mugs of coffee. They would often tell their waiter to leave the whole coffee pot on the table to save him the trip of constantly refilling their cups. For Mr. Brown, the buffet was the most affordable way to enjoy breakfast without breaking the bank. They would strategically sit in a corner at a half circular booth, since it was the perfect location to see every guest entering the buffet. These same guests would most likely be attending the convention as well and they liked to scope out the clientele in advance.

Mr. Brown looked up from pouring himself another cup of coffee to see Jerry following the host. He was walking to a table with his wife and another guest. Mr. Brown knew that he had to take this coincidence as a new opportunity for gaining Jerry's business. But how? He noticed that Jerry and his guests had not gone into the buffet line because they were going to order a full breakfast from the waiter. Then, he had a stroke of genius.

Sam I Am asked him what was going on because he was sitting there with the coffee pot in one hand and his mouth open, abnormally quiet. He told Sam I Am the whole story of his history with Jerry and how desperate he was to reopen that account. Then he announced, "I am going to pay for their breakfast!"

Sam I Am almost coughed up his coffee. "No way, are you serious? What about our budget?"

Mr. Brown explained that sometimes it was worth it to take a small financial risk in pursuit of something larger. But even as he made this decision, doubt entered his mind. The outcome could easily swing in either direction. They would either gain Jerry's attention or lose him altogether. Jerry might surely think, *these guys are going too far.* But sometimes going far helps you stick out from the crowd of others playing it safe.

Sam I Am moved quickly to speak to the waiter taking care of Jerry's table. Even the waiter was puzzled, but without much argument he gave him their check. They took care of the check and sat at their table anxiously waiting for the show to unfold at Jerry's table.

When Jerry and his guests were done with their food, they signaled for the waiter to bring the check. The waiter passed their table several times before Jerry seemed to lose his patience with waving at the waiter and asking for the check. From the waiter's gestures, they could tell that he was telling Jerry that it had already been taken care of. Jerry was shocked when the waiter pointed at Mr. Brown's table. He must have seen Mr. Brown's grin because he immediately started laughing. He knew from experience that Mr. Brown was always up to something. Next thing the team knew, Jerry was coming over to their table.

"What are you doing hiding in this corner watching everybody come in and out of here?" He laughed, clearly amused, "Thank you for buying me breakfast. That was unexpected." Mr. Brown said, "I never had a chance to have breakfast with you. This is the least I can do."

They chatted for five minutes and Jerry was truly touched and grateful. Our Mr. Brown requested that he be allowed to show him a few new items they were introducing at the convention. Jerry said he would see them sharply at 10:00 a.m. that day when the doors opened. With that, he left. Having heard promises from Jerry before, Mr. Brown did not want to get his hopes up.

Imagine his surprise when Jerry showed up on the dot with his wife and guest. At this point it was not important whether Jerry placed orders from them. What was important was that Mr. Brown had inspired him to keep his word and his financial risk had not gone to waste. Jerry ended up spending two hours at their booth. He went over the wide spectrum of their merchandise, taking notes of various things. Sam I Am's pen was busy writing up his orders and Mr. Brown could sense Sam I Am's satisfaction in accomplishing their goal.

After reviewing the entire selection Jerry told Sam I Am to total up the order and give him the copy. Sam I Am didn't give the total number verbally but only handed him a copy of the order. Jerry went over a couple of pages of his order with satisfaction until he finally looked at the total. He started to laugh and looked up at Mr. Brown and said, "You son of a gun. This was the single most expensive breakfast I've ever had in my life." He shook his hand with a firm grip, a solid laugh and a big hug. "Thank you once again for buying our breakfast. I'm looking forward to our friendship to come."

At this point, Sam I Am was too shocked to say anything. A few hours ago, neither him nor Mr. Brown had thought that such a positive outcome could have been the result of such a small gesture. Let's continue with another interesting breakfast story.

Tennessee and Alabama - November

Mr. Lewis was an old timer in his early seventies. He was a real genuine southerner, an honest man of word and principle. Once he began to speak, you had better pay attention. If you didn't focus on what he was saying he would already be on to the next thought before you got the chance to catch up. He spoke at a very fast speed for his age. He was a slick businessman too and Mr. Brown was unsuccessful numerous times in trying to meet and sell to him. Mr. Lewis always had his schedule planned long in advance and Mr. Brown knew that his only chance was to throw him off his usual routine and surprise him somehow.

Before the holiday season started that year, Mr. Brown decided to meet a few clients in the southern states. He ended up in Tennessee, one of his favorite states for both business and travel. After meeting a client, he found himself free and ahead of schedule. It was Friday and he realized he was not only free for the rest of the day, but also the next morning. Since he wasn't flying out of Nashville until late in the evening on Saturday, his goal was to make the best use of his time and money before flying back home. Rather than gallivant around the city he decided to try his luck with the slippery Mr. Lewis, who lived in Decatur, Alabama. This was going to be a totally blind call, but it could be his chance to finagle an opening in Mr. Lewis's schedule.

When Mr. Lewis himself came on the line, Mr. Brown said, "Mr. Lewis, I am on the border of Tennessee and Alabama. Please allow me to visit you and give me thirty minutes of your time. I can stop by before your doors open for business tomorrow."

"Tomorrow," he said dismissively, "Hell no. It's Saturday, I cannot see you. I do not allow anyone to see me or sell me anything on the weekend."

As always, Mr. Brown didn't want to take no for an answer. "Mr. Lewis," he said again, "You can set the timer. Just throw me out once the 30th minute is over. I assure you I will not disappoint you. Please sir?"

To our Mr. Brown's surprise, Mr. Lewis reluctantly said,

"Okay, come sharply at 8:30 a.m. tomorrow morning and I will give you exactly 30 minutes. Do not be disappointed if you do not get an order from me." Without hesitation, Mr. Brown jumped in his car and drove well over a hundred miles. He got a hotel room, ate dinner and went to bed.

The next day he was fresh and ready for that golden opportunity. Since he was new to the area he checked out of the hotel and left early. Mr. Brown would always rather be early than late. At 8:15 a.m. he reached Mr. Lewis's business. He couldn't believe that he was finally going to be meeting with him. The only time Mr. Brown had seen Mr. Lewis previously was walking past him on the buying floor.

Mr. Lewis greeted him at the entrance and offered him a coffee to take the chill off the chilly November day. Mr. Brown didn't waste any time getting down to business. As they walked in, Mr. Lewis explained that this was the first time in his life that he had allowed anyone to see him on a Saturday to sell. Mr. Brown told him how much he appreciated being given the chance to present his merchandise. As he quickly laid out his entire line, Mr. Lewis looked pleased and called in his buyer. They soon became engrossed in discussing the various pieces that had been presented. One thing led to another, and then to another, and before they knew it, an hour had passed. They hadn't even realized it until one of Mr. Lewis's clients walked in for a 10:00 a.m. appointment and greeted him. Mr. Lewis looked down at his watch before shaking the man's hand. The spell our Mr. Brown had cast over him was broken. Mr. Lewis stopped abruptly and said, "Son, your 30 minutes is over. Please pack up and write me up the order."

Mr. Brown wrote up the order, packed his displays and

prepared to leave. On his way out he noticed how warmly Mr. Lewis greeted each customer. He spoke briefly to every one of them, then made sure he directed them to the appropriate salesperson.

Before Mr. Brown left his showroom, Mr. Lewis asked, "Did I buy enough merchandise to fill up your gas tank for your return trip to Nashville?" Mr. Brown couldn't help but smile. He had indeed purchased enough for the drive back. In fact, it was enough to drive all the way back to New York City!

A couple of years passed. History was repeating itself. Mr. Brown received no more orders from Mr. Lewis. He made so many phone calls but only received the same answer: "I will keep you in mind." He didn't know what went wrong or what had happened to change his mind. He had done all he could from his side to take care of Mr. Lewis's orders. He was anxious to grab his attention again and conduct more business. He kept an eye out for him at every trade show, just waiting for an opening. With Mr. Brown's persistence the perfect opportunity eventually arrived.

As always, our Mr. Brown was having breakfast with his younger colleague, Sam I Am. The rest of the sales team was with them this time as well and they were recounting the night before and giving each other pep talks for the six-to-eight-hour trade show ahead. While Mr. Brown was talking, he saw Mr. and Mrs. Lewis enter the breakfast hall. He and Sam I am looked at each other thinking that this strategy had worked before and could work again. They read each other's minds and Sam I Am stood up. The rest of the sales team looked up curiously at his sudden departure. He went over to the waitress and paid Mr. Lewis's bill.

Mr. and Mrs. Lewis took their time eating, oblivious to the plan. The sales team waited with fingers crossed, watching to see what would happen. Soon the waitress's finger was pointing at them. Mr. Lewis looked surprised and the next thing they knew he was at their table trying to figure out what was going on. He introduced his wife and said, "Son, nice to see you again. That was a nice surprise. Thanks for buying us breakfast." They spoke briefly and before leaving he said, "I'll be seeing you in the buying hall."

Sure enough, Mr. Lewis showed up at the booth as soon as the doors opened. He inquired about what people were buying and which pieces had been the top sellers that year. He took his sweet time going through various products and seemed like he was in no hurry at all. By the time they had written up his order, it reached $38,000! Surprise, surprise indeed.

The element of surprise may seem like an odd tactic, but it can certainly work in your favor. The whole idea is to do the unexpected and to think on your feet. Just because someone has denied you in the past does not mean they will do so forever. People change, economies change, circumstances change. By embracing spontaneity and trying new things you might even surprise yourself!

Over time, Mr. Brown's team has supplied over $300,000 worth of merchandise and counting to Jerry. It goes to show how you must cash in on every possible opportunity that comes your way. No matter how small the opportunity, just take it, because it could be the opening of a new door and a lasting business relationship. It could also be the cementing of a stronger bond with an already existing client, which in turn, takes the business to new heights. None of that would have happened if Mr. Brown had not trusted his instincts and taken advantage of an opportunity at breakfast.

Mr. Brown continued doing business with Mr. Lewis making sales that eventually totaled $200,000 and counting. In fact, he is still a client to this day. That story proves that there isn't a single human being who does not appreciate a *pleasant* little surprise or unexpected gesture, especially if it brings them joy.

What did you do to surprise someone today?

THE WRAP UPS – BY MR. BROWN

- *Big returns can come with small investments.*
- *Do not start your day with an empty stomach, always keep the engine running.*
- *Everyone loves a pleasant surprise.*

If a stranger invites you to go home with them, would you?

What is the value of trust?
What price tag would you put on it?

What service do you provide that differentiates you from your competitors?

Do you cover your ears when advice comes from the younger generation?

Have you ever put your feet into a customer's shoes and felt their pain?

Has anyone ever betrayed your trust?

Mr. Brown encountered these challenges as part of doing business. The next chapters will show you his experiences and how he combated these complex circumstances.

DAILY EXPERIENCES IN BUSINESS

What do you have that the other person does not have? With the arrival of the internet, things have changed drastically. The world has become a very small and competitive place. The old-fashioned way of doing business is diminishing and becoming a thing of the past. This is true in most any industry. In other words, any activity where there is an interaction between two parties, you need to be different and think outside the box.

Let's go a step further and ask the same question in the business world. What does your business have to offer that your competitor cannot give? It is not only the products that you sell, but the combination of your honest, genuine, sincere approach topped off with excellent customer service. These traits will differentiate you from your competitors.

The following stories are connected to customer care, customer service, sales growth and how to get your foot into a closed door. Today the biggest challenge is to open new doors in business, earn loyalty, increase customer retention and ultimately gain sales growth.

Read and observe how far, and to what extent, one goes to draw customer attention, attract customers, win them over and earn their business and loyalty. Think, analyze and decide for yourself if you would have acted in similar or different fashion. The low or not cost wrap up lessons learned are very simple to follow and easy to put into practice.

WHY SHOULD I BUY FROM YOU?

Do you have an answer?

WHY SHOULD I BUY FROM YOU?

"Price is not the only quotient." – Mr. Brown

The questions above are both simple and humble. They are ones you probably ask yourself daily. You ask when you go grocery shopping, shop for a new car, renew an insurance policy, open a new bank account, etc. The answer to these questions varies, but you are sure to encounter them in all walks of life.

Now let's turn the table. You are the entrepreneur running the business. Do you have an answer? You had better, because any prospective client would like to know the answer. You don't have time to think and then answer. You must be prepared. If you do not have an answer on the spot, you will look like a fool in their eye. So, you are better off doing your homework. This is especially true for anyone just starting out in the business world.

Take the time to figure out what your strengths are. Where do you stand in comparison to your best competitor? How can the client benefit from using your services over your competition? What is it about you and your services that will benefit the client by using you? How are you going to save or make them money? Once you know what you have to offer, you will be more than prepared to make a would-be client into a lifelong one. I wanted to satisfy my curiosity, so I decided to ask Mr. Brown for his answers.

New York, New York - Spring

To answer my question, Mr. Brown started to flip through his address book, which is at least twenty-five years old, to find the perfect story for me. According to Mr. Brown, Seymour was one of the finest gentlemen he'd ever come across and much like Debbie, his word of mouth was more powerful than any signed agreement. One afternoon Mr. Brown had gone to Seymour's office to take care of some business. After finishing their discussion Seymour asked, "So who is your insurance advisor?" Mr. Brown was puzzled because this question had no relevance to the business at hand. After telling him the name of his broker and the insurance company Seymour said, "Let me give you a piece of advice, like I would to my son. There are a lot of insurance companies out there. They will give you lower premiums, but the most important thing is the service they will render if an accident were to occur. It is of utmost importance that your agent is knowledgeable and thorough in what he's selling." Mr. Brown listened intently as he went on. "The agent may be a bit expensive, but it is worth paying that little extra for peace of mind that will let you sleep easy at night. I am sure a man like you has a good agent. However, if you are interested, I can recommend mine. He is the best I have come across in my over forty years of experience."

With nothing to lose and everything to gain from Seymour's suggestion, Mr. Brown took advantage of the opportunity and agreed to speak to his agent. But more important than the invaluable advice was the way Seymour had presented it to him. His pitch for the agent's services had been incredibly effective. Mr. Brown knew that sooner or later he would encounter a situation where a buyer would ask a simple question "Why should I buy from you?" He wanted to deliver as smooth and convincing an explanation as Seymour had given him. Sure enough, that day did arrive.

Mr. Brown was traveling in San Antonio, Texas where he met a CEO named Charlie. After reviewing his merchandise, the first question Charlie asked was, "Why should I buy from you? You are not the only supplier in this industry. Moreover, you are a bit pricey. "

Mr. Brown thought of Seymour and prepared his articulate answer. "I may not be the lowest price, but I am not overcharging you. However, if you were to call me on the 22nd of December for any merchandise that you may need for Christmas, I will make sure to deliver it. I will not hesitate to take care of a client who is counting on me, even if it means losing some money on the deal. I would rather develop a long-term business relationship with you than a short-term one." Charlie was a savvy businessman. He realized the future potential. Mr. Brown earned Charlie's business and his trust.

The conversation with Seymour really paid off. Here he was, prepared for a question that Charlie and others like him probably asked all the time. He was able to provide the answer as to why he was priced higher than other suppliers, also assuring Charlie that his was a reliable firm. And all because his buddy Seymour had shown him that price is not everything. Peace of mind is invaluable.

THE WRAP UPS – BY MR. BROWN

- *When you compete on price, there is no floor.*
- *Clients will pay for peace of mind.*

CHAPTER

12

FED UP

How do you change the game?

FED UP

"A satisfied customer is always the best advertiser." – Mr. Brown

---

Would you rather work with someone who is boring or someone who keeps you at the edge of your seat waiting to see what comes next? We all know business can get monotonous once it becomes routine, eventually, it becomes boring. You could say business is like bland food. If you continue to always eat your favorite dish the same way, over time even it will become boring and you will begin to dislike it all together. If that happens do you know what you can do to fix it? Spice it up. It's that simple. Enhance the flavor to enjoy a new version of your favorite dish. Everyone around you will wonder how it is that you are still enjoying the same old thing after all this time. Similarly, add humor and smile in and around business to spice it up. Your business interactions will feel lighter and you will have smooth sailing. So, the choice is yours: either you can make business fun, or you can continue trudging through, doing the same bland routine every day.

Once you get used to this new process you will find that you can have serious discussions with a touch of humor. In fact, that evening meeting will always be remembered as a most memorable and pleasurable one you shared with them. I'm telling you; people just love humor. Mr. Brown was always the first to try to add humor to every situation and sometimes even make a fool of himself in order to win over clients. Quite a few of his clients were won over during laughter. And imagine how happy his team was over such low cost no brainers. Listen, anyone can spend money to get attention and recognition, but to be recognized without paying a dime you need to be creative and playful. You need to think and look beyond the normal bland four walls of a box.

Smyrna, Georgia - Smyrna Convention Center - Summer Show

Speaking of thinking and looking different beyond the four walls of a box, how many of you would wear a baseball hat with a suit and tie while conducting business at a tradeshow? Mr. Brown absolutely loves baseball hats and will wear them while working at a trade show or while traveling. He always wears baseball hats no matter the season. Rich also loved wearing baseball hats.

Rich had multiple megastore operations in and around Columbia, South Carolina. Mr. Brown never had the chance to meet with him until he was in one of the shows at the Smyrna Convention Center. No one could miss Rich when he arrived in the buying hall. He was over six feet tall! Rich and his team spent three days in meetings with their vendors while making sure to accomplish everything they needed to for the holiday season. Mr. Brown knew this because he had observed Rich for over eight years, trying to figure out how he could fit in a chance moment to gain his attention. Unfortunately, he always failed miserably and had no chance in getting Rich to his booth. After all, Rich was very loyal to his vendors with which he was already booked and that was one thing that Mr. Brown had always liked about him. Mr. Brown refused to let those eight years of failing affect him. He continued to hope and sure enough, his patience was rewarded.

One day during that Summer Show, Mr. Brown saw that Rich and his team were seated and working with one of their vendors down the aisle. Mr. Brown was hoping for some miracle or chance of luck. He was so close to him, yet so far away! This time his luck came in the form of his loyal client and dear friend Michelle, a southern belle from Eden, North Carolina. She ran a very successful multi-store operation in North Carolina and Virginia.

Michelle always came prepared with her shopping list on the first day at the first hour to get all her purchases made early at Mr. Brown's booth. Though they had already done business on the opening day, today she was leaving so she had come by to wish him well before she left. They chit-chatted for a little while when, from out of the blue, she recognized a friend of hers. "By the way," she said, "do you know that gentleman?"

Mr. Brown couldn't believe his ears. She was pointing at Rich! He hadn't even been a point of discussion. She had come out of nowhere with the question. Of course, Mr. Brown jumped at the chance to meet him. After saying, "Give me a minute," Michelle went straight up to Rich, said something that made him get up from his chair, and holding his hand like a little boy, brought him to Mr. Brown's booth for an introduction. She told Rich which deals she had purchased and suggested that he should return to the booth later with his team and go over the same great deals. Rich agreed and returned once he was done with his business at the other booth. That was a golden moment for Mr. Brown. He had to take advantage of that opportunity presented to him! If he blew it, there wouldn't be a second chance. He would be history.

Rich was a fun guy and asked, "So, it seems you like hats?" He went on challenging him saying that the only way he would look at Mr. Brown's merchandise was if he agreed to wear a baseball cap of his favorite team, the South Carolina Gamecocks. Mr. Brown agreed saying that he most definitely would put on the hat. Rich promptly pulled one red Gamecock hat from his bag and gave it to him. Rich had clearly come prepared, so without any hesitation or thoughts about where the hat had been, Mr. Brown wore it with a smile. Rich stood there with a huge grin on his face alongside his entire buying team. Marilyn, who oversaw managing Rich's business, was also there. She agreed it was a good idea to take advantage of the deals and agreed to place a sample order.

It took less than a year for Rich and Marilyn to build up confidence in Mr. Brown, his team, his firm and his entire support team in the office. Everything they wanted had always been delivered as promised and all the orders that he sent via fax were shipped either the same day or the next day. It only took three years before they had touched their first million dollars in sales together. That red hat was the catalyst responsible for his patronage. Their business has only grown larger since. Rich was able to spot Mr. Brown from a distance because, as promised, he proudly wore the Gamecock hat and was the only red hat head on the entire convention show floor!

The hat was a real game changer and a red traffic light for other clients as well. People would stop in his booth to ask Mr. Brown if he was a Gamecocks fan, and those who were living in the Tennessee and Georgia area were especially curious about it. How's that for advertising? The hat made it even more fun because he never knew what kind of greeting, he would get. It was not always a happy greeting! Lots of folks hated that he was wearing the hat of their rival team. Either way, the red hat did nothing but open doors for Mr. Brown. He safely concluded that it was the red Gamecocks hat that had been one of his most successful sales team members.

New York City, New York - Mr. Brown's Office

The only other people I know of who wear hats more often are those who work for delivery services. Mr. Brown realized this as well and decided to run with an idea. The shipping services he used in his business were FedEx and UPS. In the evening, UPS and FedEx would always pick up their corresponding shipments from his office. Both the company's delivery people would always come in wearing their respective company hats.

An idea started to take shape in his mind. Why not create a hat saying "FEDUP?" Or create a hat that said "UPS" in front and "FedEx" on the back, or vice versa? Or, maybe one of his team members could wear a UPS hat and the other a FedEx hat! The possibilities were fun to consider, and they decided to go with the latter concept.

The idea was to help two different team members at trade shows strike up two different conversations with already existing or potentially new clients. It's human nature to be curious and inquisitive. As the saying goes, curiosity killed the cat, but satisfaction brought it back. Would there be any curious cats in the aisles of the trade show?

At first, the only reaction they got was a few people laughing as they walked past the booth. As the hours went by, people started asking what was going on? The answer was always the same as they had rehearsed. "How do you want your merchandise shipped? UPS or FedEx? You have a choice." The answer made the people laugh even more since these were the same services everyone else used. The strategy ended up being an excellent conversation starter striking conversation after conversation.

Once a prospective client smiles or laughs, you have succeeded in breaking the ice. The team had won half the battle of getting someone's attention just by wearing the hats. The next step was to go speak to them and convince them to look at their merchandise. Even if you fail to close a sale, no problem. At least you have the satisfaction of bringing in the clients to the booth and leaving an impression they'll hopefully remember, knowing you had presented them with the entire line. Now you could go ahead and hope for that fruitful fortune in a follow up phone call or order.

THE WRAP UPS – BY MR. BROWN

- *Vendor loyalty always pays off in the long run.*
- *Humor and a smile are the spice of business deals.*
- *Be proud to be the mascot of your company.*

CHAPTER

13

RUN BROWN MAN RUN

Do you love your customer?

RUN BROWN MAN RUN

"Always bring your running shoes to work." – Mr. Brown

"I will keep you in mind. You have some great products to offer." How many of you as a supplier or service provider heard those words from a prospective client for years accompanied by the sound of the door closing behind you? How many of you have lost patience after a few attempts and have crossed a potential client off your list? Here is a very interesting story from the collection of Mr. Brown's business experiences when forces of patience, persistence, customer service and a little luck collided. Closed doors were popped open.

This story is about Mr. Berkeley from Oklahoma City, OK - a highly sophisticated businessman in his late sixties who kept his door closed when it came to buying product from our Mr. Brown, no matter how hard he tried to attract his interest. Mr. Berkeley would always entertain him, allowing him to present merchandise in the conference room of his office. When it came time to place an order with pen and paper, Mr. Berkeley would inevitably say, "I will keep you in mind. You have some great products to offer." Then the encounter would end with the door closing soundly behind Mr. Brown on his way out.

Oklahoma City, Oklahoma - Mr. Berkeley's Showroom

The same scene unfolded for a few years, but Mr. Brown did not lose patience or hope. Every time he would go to Oklahoma, he would call Mr. Berkeley. Sure enough, one day that office door stayed propped open instead of closed shut; Mr. Berkeley seemed more genuinely interested in the merchandise presented. So, you can only imagine Mr. Brown's annoyance when suddenly, his phone started ringing in the middle of reviewing merchandise. Mr. Brown saw that it was his New York office and they knew to never call unless it was urgent. Reluctantly, he asked Mr. Berkeley if he could be excused.

It turned out that it really was an urgent matter—an important business arrangement had been made and Mr. Brown had a product in his sample line that needed to be shipped immediately for Next Day Air Delivery. It would have been easy for him to object and say it was not possible to ship as it was already around 5:30 p.m. in New York and UPS and FedEx had already picked up shipments by 5:00 p.m. The easiest answer to the customer would have been, "We appreciate your call and order, but it's way too late to ship. The earliest shipment will be tomorrow." By now, you all know as much as I do how much Mr. Brown hates the word NO, so instead he told the office to fax a document to Oklahoma, then asked Mr. Berkeley if he could use some paper and an empty box to ship a package. Mr. Berkeley told him it was no problem and that he would be happy to help.

In those days, Mr. Brown would carry blank UPS and FedEx shipping labels and packages so he could ship anything he had to any client in the United States. Since he had an account set up with both companies, all he needed was a fax from the office for information about the merchandise to be shipped. It was that simple.

He told Mr. Berkeley that he would be right back. Mr. Berkeley looked at him curiously. He had no idea what he was up to, or what was going on. Mr. Brown headed to his car with his box of merchandise and the documents that had been faxed over, placed the box in the UPS envelope, sealed it, and slapped on the shipping label. He pulled out of his parking spot and started looking for a brown UPS truck. He wanted to hand it to the delivery man himself. It was a little past 4:45 p.m. in Oklahoma, so he still had a chance to find one making deliveries.

Finally, he spotted one on the main road and thought to himself, *Run Brown Man run!* He pulled out behind the UPS truck thinking it would stop soon to either deliver or pick up. He planned to catch up with the driver and hand him or her the package so that he knew it would be on the truck in time for the next day delivery. Unfortunately, the driver continued down the main road not pulling off anywhere along the way. For five minutes, Mr. Brown did his best to get the driver's attention from directly behind the truck, flashing his high beams and waving out the window.

Back at Mr. Berkeley's office, the very man he had spent so much time and effort trying to sell to was waiting for him, but Mr. Brown knew he had to get the package shipped before he could proceed with Mr. Berkeley. The client who'd called the office in New York had promised his retail customer that it would be there the next day—the customer wanted to give the gift to a loved one and it was imperative that it arrived in time. As always, Mr. Brown put himself in his client's shoes, vowing to make this happen.

Suddenly, the UPS truck took a turn off the main road and started going towards the airport. Mr. Brown was beginning to panic; he had no clue where this chase would end. The van entered a big building, which he soon recognized as a UPS shipping facility! Mr. Brown was so glad that he'd stuck to his guns and followed the driver. Now that he was at the actual facility, he knew for certain that the package would go out that day. He jumped out of his car and ran to the driver to give him the package. The driver looked at him in shock and then at the package: "So that was *you* flashing high beams at me! It was for me to stop! Brother, I am truly sorry. It never occurred to me that a package was the reason." He scanned the package and gave him the receipt.

At that moment, no one in this world could measure just how happy Mr. Brown felt. The item that the customer selected was now being shipped from the sample line, specifically for him, from across the country. As Mr. Brown drove back to Mr. Berkeley's, he called the New York office and gave them the tracking number so that everyone's minds would be put at ease.

When he returned to Mr. Berkeley's he was a bit out of breath, as if he really had been running after the van. As Mr. Brown recounted the entire story, Mr. Berkeley couldn't believe that Mr. Brown had gone to such extreme measures to satisfy a client, and he began to rethink his own approach to business.

Mr. Berkeley invited him to relax in the conference room with the rest of his team where, to Mr. Brown's utmost surprise, they placed a sizeable order. Pen was finally hitting paper! A genuine breakthrough and Mr. Brown hadn't even been trying to impress him; he'd simply stuck to his guns and provided his usual standard of customer service.

Mr. Berkeley became one of Mr. Brown's best clients, as well as a close friend. After that, he and his wife would come to Las Vegas and visit Mr. Brown at the trade show every year. He would always arrive on Monday in the afternoon, the day before the show's end. After reviewing the entire line with his wife, he would place orders for the holidays.

Before leaving the buying hall he would set up dinner for the following day around 7:00 p.m. same time, same place at Bally's Chinese restaurant.

Their business and friendship lasted for many years until Mr. Berkeley lost his wife. She had been instrumental in the growth of Mr. Berkeley's business and he was shocked to lose her. After that, he had little motivation left to run the business and it became too much for him to handle. Eventually, he decided to close and brought down the curtain in December of 2004. Mr. Brown wholeheartedly supported his closing sale by shipping him a large quantity of merchandise. He did his best to try to find him after his business closed, but Mr. Berkeley disappeared. He still misses chasing him.

THE WRAP UPS – BY MR. BROWN

- *Run the extra mile to take care of your customer.*
- *Remember your oldest clients made you what you are today, always respect them.*
- *Always be prepared to run with the right materials to foster a sale.*

CHAPTER

14

PLEASE ALLOW ME TO

Have you ever had an angry customer?

PLEASE ALLOW ME TO

"Often, a simple phrase can close a long-winded sale – Mr. Brown

---

No one can deny the fact that we are living in one of the most competitive environments of all time. Especially with the use of technology, competitors are watching our every move. Make one mistake and they will swoop in to eat you and your business alive. You can have the best products to sell, but if your marketing or sales team is weak, even the best product will go down the drain. It will be overshadowed by the company that is giving a better performance and presentation. So how can you continue surprising clients and stay ahead in the game?

Take it from Mr. Brown who one-ups his competitors respectfully. He has practiced, insisted and instituted his business methods into his entire firm. He aims to have his clients experience the same level of service no matter who they speak to in his firm. They do this by throwing out the boring stuff so doing business with their firm is fun as well as fruitful. Give a client the service that they want and deserve. They will be willing to pay a little extra for a superior service.

Using a phrase as simple as "Please allow me to" can make a client feel comfortable and make the experience more memorable. This pleasant experience, in turn, differentiates Mr. Brown's business from the rest of the crowd. How many times do you come across a business where every department is on the same level of customer service no matter who you talk to? In addition, how many businesses can claim with pride that their clients say, "You guys are easy to work with and you make our lives easier?" Not many.

Gatlinburg, Tennessee - Holiday Season

The art of using the right phrase at the right time was one our Mr. Brown learned while observing a good friend and client named Robert, who operated his business out of the mountain resort city of Gatlinburg, Tennessee. During holidays or weekends, tourists flock to the Smoky Mountains and stayed in one of Gatlinburg's many cabins, chalets, condos or bed and breakfasts. Many tourists, especially those coming in for the Winterfest Celebration, wanted to buy something, but couldn't make up their minds. Unless a salesperson is a mind reader, it's often hard to convince tourists they should purchase their merchandise.

On this occasion, Robert's store was jam-packed with tourists and Mr. Brown was standing out of the way waiting for him to finish work. As he waited, he started observing how each sales associate was handling the client. It seemed as if none of the young sales team members had even finished college, yet they had picked up the basic skills of persuasion, presentation and the convincing power necessary to close a sale. Robert himself was engrossed with a few clients. It had been over an hour and they still hadn't decided what to buy. Robert finally said, "Ladies, no offense to you, but I have shown you nearly my entire collection. What will it take for me to do to earn your business? How can I help you, please tell me?" Mr. Brown was stunned to hear this from Robert. What an honest way to persuade an undecided shopper to make a purchase.

The ladies looked at each other for a moment. One of them reluctantly replied, "We have a budget and though we like your products, they are a bit expensive. It's a stretch in our budget for the items we're interested in." It seemed

> Robert's statement had encouraged her to speak, and boy did it have a positive effect.
>
> Robert replied without hesitation, "I am glad you told me! Please allow me to do this for you. I will make a special deal and take 10% off your purchase." He then added whispering, "I'll also throw in some coupons for free ice cream next door for all of you. It's on me." The ladies cracked up and took another look at the merchandise.
>
> After closing the sale, Robert explained his sales technique to the intrigued Mr. Brown, stating that he often used the phrase "What will it take for me to do to earn your business?" when selling to indecisive shoppers. Here was a simple yet effective phrase that asked, in a polite way, how can I really help you? Mr. Brown immediately put this into his business practice and found that nine out of ten times, undecided folks would divulge what was holding them back. If they were still feeling hesitant or indecisive, he would use "Please allow me to" as an additional incentive, generous offer or simply a polite manner of speaking. As we have learned, once the customer tells you the truth, the ball is in your court.

A happily satisfied customer can act as an excellent ambassador for your brand, so the more tricks you have up your sleeve to keep a customer happy, the better. Though small, "Please allow me to" or "How can I help" are potent phrases that make the customer feel heard, respected and catered to. Word of mouth is the least expensive way to promote a business, and if everyone who comes in your door leaves with a smile, they'll be sure to recommend you.

Here are some phrases that Mr. Brown and his team have personally found effective:

> "Please allow me to find out what can be done."
>
> "Please allow me to get back to you."
>
> "Please allow me to find out for you."

Mr. Brown went so far as to give all his sales team members clear instructions to use these phrases, because it is important for the same values of a company to be reflected at all levels of the business. In addition to using these phrases, Mr. Brown or any sales team member who is not occupied on the sales floor at a convention or show is encouraged to greet potential customers with some dry snacks, like mixed nuts and a napkin. It's important to treat clients and prospective clients as guests. Wouldn't you welcome and treat guests at home by offering them a snack?

But no business model runs smoothly all the time. Sometimes a client will complain to Mr. Brown on the phone that someone was supposed to call back but never did. On the rare occasion when this happens, the foundation on which he created his business appears to be shaking.

Apologizing profusely, he will tell them, "Please allow me to get back to you in five minutes. I will make sure I drop everything and take care of the problem immediately or assign the job to someone for immediate action." He always diffuses a stressful moment by giving assurance to a client that a reply is on the way. By solving the problem, fighting negativity with positivity, and providing excellent service, the client will be with you for the long run. And even if they do leave for whatever reason beyond your control, they will always remember the efficiency, promptness and warm service your firm offered in the past.

THE WRAP UPS – BY MR. BROWN

- *Do not underestimate the power of a simple phrase.*
- *Be adaptive and always be willing to learn, even if the lesson comes from a younger generation.*
- *Don't ever use, "Wait a sec, let me find out." It sounds cheap and unprofessional.*

CHAPTER

15

I FEEL YOU BROTHA'

Have you ever thought of yourself as a Santa?

I FEEL YOU BROTHA'

"Your pain is my pain." – Mr. Brown

When someone goes above and beyond for you, even though they don't have to, doesn't that make you want to come back for more? That kind of service is hard to find in the age of automated messages. Some apps don't even have a customer service center, but only offer automated responses. Sometimes things do not go as planned. Who will be there to lend a helping hand when you need it the most?

Lumberton, North Carolina - Holiday Season

As far back as Mr. Brown can remember, doing business with Tim started out slow, small and humble. Like everyone else, Tim had to feel comfortable and confident with Mr. Brown as a supplier before opening the door fully and gambling all in with him. But it only took one incident to change his entire perception of Mr. Brown, his firm and the service that came with it. The right shoe and the right fit.

It was Thursday, a day before Christmas Eve in 2004, when Tim called our Mr. Brown out of the blue. He explained that he needed Mr. Brown's help and to please see what he could do for him; Mr. Brown could sense his urgency. Tim was in panic mode as he explained that one of his best clients had just exited the store. This client always spent a decent amount of money during the holidays and throughout the year, but this year he had completely forgotten to place his order ahead of time. Now here was the challenge: the client wanted three pairs of 1 carat total weight each, identical diamond earrings for his three daughters. One can imagine the result of forgetting to bring a gift for a loved one, especially when that loved one happens to be a daughter (or three!). Then tack on the fact that it's Christmas!

Tim had promised this important client that he would take care of everything. Under normal circumstances, Tim could always get a product to him by the next business day. But this time, his client had totally thrown him for a loop. The products had to be identical in quality and value. After the client left, Tim felt lost. All he knew was that the ball was in his court and that the time bomb had started ticking. And so, he had called Mr. Brown and explained the entire situation, not so calmly. Mr. Brown didn't want to let him down and assured Tim that his client would be taken care of. Even though he suspected that Tim had only called him as a last resort because his current main supplier must have been unable to deliver in time, Mr. Brown did not take it personally. He wanted to offer Tim the same level of service he would offer anyone. Besides, he loved a challenge.

Mr. Brown hung up the phone and sure enough was able to find identical products for Tim. Not only three of them, but six. With twenty years of experience at the time, he knew that during December, there was a backlog of shipping at every step. On top of that, sometimes Mother Nature plays a vital role in shipping and delivering. Even if a flight takes off on time, sometimes there might be a delay in landing due to snow, rain, fog, wind or poor visibility. The reverse is also true. The flight doesn't take off at all. Then you must consider the possibility that even if a flight does land on time, someone still must physically sort it out, put it on the truck and deliver it.

After considering these scenarios, Mr. Brown decided that their best bet was to ship two packages using two different carriers in hopes that at least one of them would arrive on time. Mr. Brown called Tim back within the hour saying, "Buddy, I have picked out six identical pairs of earrings for you. I have instructed my shipping department to prepare two separate invoices, two packing slips and two shipping boxes with three identical products in each box."

While Mr. Brown knew that the weather in New York was getting worse and that snow could seriously disrupt the time of shipping, Tim was dumbfounded. He became annoyed and abruptly cut him off when he heard about the double order, saying he only needed three pairs and that he did not want to pay extra for two separate shipping packages. He obviously didn't know about the messy weather conditions in New York since he was in bright and sunny North Carolina.

Mr. Brown understood Tim's irritation; anyone who works during the holiday season spends too many hours with not enough sleep and meals on the go, resulting in stress. Sensing his frustration, Mr. Brown tried to make Tim's life easier by saying, "If you get both the packages on time and on the same day, please pay shipping for only one. But if you get only one package and not the second, you pay shipping for only one and treat me to a nice dinner next time I see you to thank me for taking such good care of your valuable client."

This request was meant to cheer Tim up and make him smile. Despite his stress, Tim did his best to laugh. Mr. Brown had created a win-win situation for Tim. Either way, he would be getting all the items he requested for his client. He chuckled again, a bit more at ease, and agreed to the terms before hanging up.

Mr. Brown went to work, telling his shipping department to

ship one package through UPS and the second through FedEx Next Day Air. Since he loved a good challenge, he was excited for the turnout of these two packages and told the shipping department to track them from the moment they were picked up. It thrilled him to call Tim and give him the happy news the moment the packages were on the truck in New York. He relayed the shipping numbers, thinking of them as lottery numbers. Which one was going to win? Would he win big twice? Now the only thing left to do was hope that at least one package would arrive safely and on time for the client to pick up the next day.

Mr. Brown was enjoying the odds of the circumstances so much that he decided to turn it into a game for everyone in his office. He included his team members, one of whom offered to oversee tracking the status of both packages, even from home. Early morning the next day, the first report came via a phone call from that team member saying that both packages were en route. It was around 8:00 a.m. when Mr. Brown stepped out into the crisp cold air to walk near the ice-skating rink in Rockefeller Center. No snow yet.

As they arrived at work, each sales team member was anxious to hear the status of the packages. Both were still showing up in the system as "in transit." Phone calls were slowing down in the office as they had just a few more hours of work before closing for their Christmas break. At 8:45 a.m. one of the ladies from the shipping department informed Mr. Brown that one of the packages was out on the truck for delivery to Tim, while the other package was still showing up as "in transit." Ready to redeem a free dinner, Mr. Brown immediately called Tim, who was tracking the package too. It was now 9:00 a.m.

Sure enough, only one package made it to Tim's office. He immediately called his client and gave him the wonderful news. His second ecstatic phone call went to Mr. Brown with a thank you, a Merry Christmas, and a very Happy New Year. He was thrilled to tell Mr. Brown that the precious gifts had been wrapped up for his client's daughters. Are you wondering what happened to the other package? Well it did arrive, but only after the holidays.

Following this incident, Tim transferred most of his business to Mr. Brown's firm. It should come as no surprise that he's still a trusted client to this day. Whenever Tim has a chance to speak at a seminar, or out with a group of people, he never fails to mention what Mr. Brown did for him that holiday season. He will insist that Mr. Brown and his firm are the best people to do business with. "What good is a supplier," he'll say, "if he fails to deliver and fails to stand by you when you need him the most?"

To this day, the total business Mr. Brown earned from Tim is over $500,000 and counting. Both of their lives are very busy, but since they're early birds, they often chat on the phone in the early morning hours. Sometimes, they look back on that first bet. How many other bets have they won or lost against each other over the years? I can't say for sure, but I do know Mr. Brown has a knack for winning.

THE WRAP UPS – BY MR. BROWN

- *Don't let your ego take a blow, even if you know you're being used as a last resort.*
- *Foresee a failure and then beat it.*
- *Stepping into your client's stress is uncomfortable but ultimately rewarding.*

CHAPTER 16

SHORT-TERM THINKING, LONG-TERM LOSS

Do you blame someone else for mistakes?

SHORT-TERM THINKING, LONG-TERM LOSS

"Someone else's quick buck can
end up in your pocket." – Mr. Brown

Long-term thinking is another core policy that has led to Mr. Brown's success from day-one of his career. He has always stressed to me that one must plan for the long-term. Do not only think in the now, but into the beyond. Even seemingly short-term clients or deals can lead to future gains, though they can just as easily turn into big losses if you aren't careful.

In the following story, his short-term goal was to see his client and dear friend Mary Anne, a busy lady who was nearly impossible to catch on the phone. Mr. Brown was thrilled when he happened to get her on the line. After a brief discussion, he invited her to visit him at his New York office when she came to town for the New York Summer Show Convention later that same year. Sure enough, she showed up on his doorstep the day of the appointment. To Mr. Brown's surprise, she made a purchase close to $25,000. She asked Mr. Brown to pay her a visit to Nashville in the fall because she would need more merchandise for the holiday season.

Nashville, Tennessee - November

Meet Jack: a tall, gruff-looking old-timer who was tough as nails. Deep down, though, he was a kind-hearted man of his word. Late one evening, Jack called Mr. Brown's New York office for the very first time. He wanted to find out the quality and price of the jewelry that Mr. Brown's firm had advertised in a national magazine. He seemed a bit stressed and asked to view various samples as soon as possible, if it was not too much of a bother.

It just so happened that Jack's business was in Murfreesboro, Tennessee, about a 45-minute drive southeast of Nashville. Mr. Brown was quick to offer his services in person and said, "Instead of speaking on the phone, how about I visit you with actual merchandise that you can cherry pick from in your office, under your very own lighting?" Jack was surprised by this gesture and quickly agreed. Mr. Brown explained that he was already flying out to Nashville the next day to meet a few clients including Mary Anne. While he was there, he could meet Jack and conduct business in person. But there was one problem. Mr. Brown had already meticulously planned his trip to make the most of his time while he was in Nashville. He would be busy working all day, every day, until 5:30 p.m. He explained this to Jack, and without any hesitation, Jack said that it would be no problem for Mr. Brown to come after 6:00 p.m. if that was convenient for him.

After years of travelling, Mr. Brown told me that personal interactions always helped cement a stronger bond with clients. He was truly looking forward to meeting Jack face-to-face and adding him to his roster. He was also excited to meet him because he had great respect for people who were willing to make the effort to go above and beyond to accommodate someone else's schedule as much as he did himself.

Sure enough, Mr. Brown made it to Nashville, accomplished his business, and was at Jack's door by 6:15 p.m. Jack gave him a warm southern welcome and brought him to a glass counter near the entrance where he could lay out everything. He inspected each piece of merchandise and selected what he wanted, astonished by the quality and appreciative of the fair price. The positive vibes were flowing between them and

Jack found exactly what he'd been looking for. His purchase ended up reaching around $20,000.

After the deal was done and the goods were packed, Jack asked Mr. Brown if he would be returning to Nashville before the holiday season was over. He went on to say that he had only purchased merchandise to fill in for now and that he would need more closer to the holidays. Of course, that was not a problem. Mr. Brown promised that he would make it back to Tennessee at least twice, though he had a nagging suspicion that the whole situation was too good to be true. Jack had just made a significant purchase and wanted to make another soon? What was the catch?

Here was a well-respected and rated retailer with a fabulous reputation making a purchase from someone he'd never met prior to that day. Why had he called the office to ask for specific merchandise? What happened to his existing suppliers?

Although any vendor would have jumped at the chance to snag this account, Mr. Brown decided to voice his concerns and ask Jack to solve the puzzle. "Come with me," Jack said with a bit of emotion. He took him to the empty front showcase. "Look inside these empty showcases at the small pieces of glass that remain. Robbers came and broke these showcases. They stole everything that was here on display. I am going into the busy prime time selling season and I need to have the whole case restocked. I cannot sell from an empty wagon. I called my supplier, whom I've been working with for over fifteen years, after the incident."

Fifteen years with the same supplier? Mr. Brown thought. Some marriages do not last half as long! He respected Jack's integrity and loyalty to his supplier.

Jack went on to say that he told the same story to his supplier, requesting replacement merchandise as soon as possible. When he inspected the merchandise he received, he realized that they were not the same goods as the ones he always ordered. In fact, he was paying the same price for lower quality merchandise! To put it simply, he was being ripped off and overcharged. The supplier, however, insisted that the goods were no different than before. But Jack was no fool. He couldn't believe that fifteen years of trust could shatter like glass in a matter of minutes. In this desperate circumstance, the supplier not only failed, but might have been trying to take advantage of Jack's situation.

Jack immediately packed all the goods and shipped them right back. He was furious and decided to cut all ties with the supplier. That was when Mr. Brown had come into the picture. While browsing through a magazine, Jack stumbled upon Mr. Brown's ad. Oddly enough, the only person to inquire about the ad that year was Jack!

Before Mr. Brown left the appointment, Jack said, "Make me the first stop on your trip when you come back, please." Mr. Brown was more than willing to help Jack in any way he could. Jack thanked him again for coming in person and their business relationship was cemented on the spot.

Over time, Mr. Brown continued doing business with Jack. He always wanted to see Mr. Brown at 6:30 a.m. before his office staff arrived, and he brewed a fresh pot of coffee bright and early. So did his son, Bill. Bill followed his father's footsteps step for step. Eventually, Bill and his sister joined the business and were just as wonderful to work with. Dad had instituted a great sense of discipline before taking a step back. I was glad to hear that absolutely nothing

> had changed even when the second generation entered the game. It was always the same early morning visit at 6:30 a.m. with a fresh pot of coffee. Mr. Brown sold at least a million dollars of merchandise to the family.
>
> Now here comes the best part. Bill kept the ball rolling and introduced Mr. Brown to a client from Columbia, Tennessee. Funny thing was that Mr. Brown knew Columbia very well. In fact, for over seven years, he'd been trying hard to break in with that same client from Columbia. It had taken Bill just one phone call and suddenly the door swung open for a visit. The client from Columbia went on to introduce him to two more clients. It's hard to keep track of how many more emerged from that single moment of long-term thinking.

As I retell the story of Jack, I am left with one conclusion: his original supplier had only been thinking on a short-term basis, and in doing so, cut short his long-term gain. This supplier missed out because Mr. Brown's long-term gain just kept gaining and gaining! And to think it all started with a short visit to Mary Anne in Nashville, a plan that led to a long and prosperous visit to the state of Tennessee.

Warning:

It is virtually impossible to break in a new solid client, unless you have something that nobody has. If Mr. Brown had been in the same situation as Jack's previous supplier, especially since they had done business with him for fifteen years, he would have said something like, "No I don't have the same quality, please give me some time and I will be sure to get it to you. In the meantime, please allow me to ship you a lower quality at a lower price if that is alright with you?" There's always an answer to a problem when you look for one. It may not be the best answer, but some sort of answer is better than to take advantage of someone's bad situation.

THE WRAP UPS – BY MR. BROWN

- *Someone's failure is your gainer, so jump up and act on it.*
- *Trust is a rare and priceless commodity in business.*
- *Never take advantage of someone in a bad situation.*

CHAPTER 17

THIS DAMN COFFEE

Has a cop ever helped you close a sale?

THIS DAMN COFFEE

"Coffee is a universal icebreaker." – Mr. Brown

Moore, Oklahoma - Fall

I don't know if you have ever been to Moore, Oklahoma, but let me tell ya, it seems like the folk there grow as tall as their corn stalks! Bo was one of those strong six-foot-tall men from Oklahoma, as stubborn and sturdy as an ox. He had a successful business and he barely had time to take query phone calls. It is always hard to find a good client, let alone an honest, respectable, good-paying client like Bo. When Bo came along, salespeople tried their hardest to get his attention. Mr. Brown and his team were unable to wrangle him in. There was no tipping him when he was sleepy. He just would not budge. One of Mr. Brown's colleagues, John, was determined to tame the famed bull, but Bo's attention was hard for John to grasp as well. And so, John's adventure in wrangling began.

It was a chilly fall day. When John called Bo, he was given an equally chilly greeting. He asked for just five minutes of Bo's time to come and present his catalogue and drop off some material for future reference. Remembering one of Mr. Brown's stories, John joked that he would even set a timer. Fortunately, John happened to catch Bo on an off day and he reluctantly agreed to the "five minutes only" meeting. John could not believe his ears!

He quickly booked a flight into Oklahoma City. After a good night's sleep, he knew he would also need some extra energy for his meeting with Bo. He went to the nearest diner to have coffee and a quick breakfast. The drive thru was crowded but the sitting area wasn't, so John decided to just eat inside, even though he was in a hurry. He sat at the window enjoying his breakfast when some unusual activity in the parking lot caught his attention. There had been some commotion and police cars were coming in. A couple officers were even out of their cars already. He quickly finished his breakfast, asked for a refill coffee to go, and grabbed his backpack. He wanted to leave before the drama slowed him down.

The moment John stepped outside, the police turned to him and told him to put up his hands or they would shoot him on the spot! They began to circle him like in a movie. It felt so surreal that for a second he thought about pinching himself to see if he was dreaming, but he didn't dare move a muscle. Now all the police officers were getting out of their cars and coming towards him.

John felt the need to speak up, saying, "What's wrong? What's the matter?"

One policeman shouted, "Turn around, hands where I can see them! Where's your car? We need to check it and inspect your backpack!"

John had no idea what was going on. They took him to sit in the back of a police car as they started to search his backpack and inspect his car. They opened the trunk, going through various papers and inspecting his carry-on bag and other random things he'd forgotten he even had in there. Reality set in when he realized that one of the policemen had a gun pointed at him the whole time. It must have been only ten minutes, but John's heart was pounding so hard it felt like hours.

Finally, the police put away their guns and suddenly it was

as if nothing had happened. They apologized profusely and asked where he was going. Totally confused, he explained that he was on the way to see Bo. It turned out that the police knew Bo from his active involvement in the community. They told John they would gladly escort him there so that he could pass all the red lights.

John worked up enough courage to ask what was going on, hoping to find a reason for the raid on his belongings. They explained that there had been trouble a couple weeks back at the restaurant and that John had fit the description of the thief. When the manager saw John coming in for breakfast, he thought the thief was back for more, so he called the police. Apparently, the thief had worn a similar shirt and hat, as well as a backpack. A classic case of mistaken identity.

John felt a little better after hearing that. He got in his car and started to relax as his heartbeat slowed to a normal pace. He tried to put the instance behind him and focus on what he was going to say to Bo. Remember, he only had five minutes of his time.

His mind stopped spinning when he reached his destination and saw the look on Bo's face. Clearly, he hadn't expected a police escort! John made his way to the open door, then paused to wave a thank you to the police for getting him to the appointment on time.

In silence, John and Bo walked up the back stairs of the store, up to the second floor where there was a kitchen area. He wasn't sure how to explain why he had shown up with police and Bo was too confused for words. Bo's wife, Peggy, was seated with some of their associates, who were eating breakfast. Peggy came forward and offered John a cup of coffee with a smile. He couldn't help but laugh.

Peggy looked at him quizzically as he continued laughing. Pointing at the cup, John explained, "A damn cup of coffee created all of that mess!" Bo told John to make himself comfortable. He wanted to satisfy his curiosity of why the cops were escorting John. He sat down to tell everyone in the room about his surreal morning. They all had a laugh and were now in great moods, ready to start the workday.

Bo gave John more coffee as a joke and asked if he could lay out his entire sample line. John smiled and kept his mouth shut about his promise for a-five-minute meeting. Maybe Bo had forgotten. Before he knew it, the five-minute mark had long passed, and he was walking out the door with a sizeable order and a bunch of new friends. Bo and his entire sales team had been surprisingly impressed and hadn't even noticed the time. The morning was filled with laughter, all because of one damn cup of coffee.

From then on, Bo and Peggy never looked at a clock again with John. He ended up earning over $250,000 in sales with Bo over the years, and the pen's gate has yet to shut. It's an invigorating feeling to do business with an ox! John found himself forever grateful to those police, since their escort helped him catch Bo's attention. As for coffee, John never looked at a cup of it the same way again.

THE WRAP UPS – BY MR. BROWN

- *Customers are not won without breaking a sweat.*
- *Even bad situations can be curbed in your favor.*
- *See bull headed prospects as a fun challenge.*

CHAPTER

18

HARNESS THE POWER OF FEAR

What are you afraid of?

HARNESS THE POWER OF FEAR

"Make fear your new best friend." – Mr. Brown

New York City, New York

The years 2008 and 2009 brought nothing but fear because the great recession had taken a toll on the masses and every industry was tightening their belts. From CEOs to hourly workers, anyone and everyone might be handed the pink slip of termination at any moment. No one could predict which direction things would move. With the stock market in freefall like the crash of 1929, every new day was a challenge. Employers were desperately trying to hold onto what they had, doing everything they could think of to keep their doors open. Mr. Brown's firm was no exception. Instead of succumbing to fear, Mr. Brown and his firm embraced this pressure to go big or go bust.

Our Mr. Brown did not let anyone, or anything spoil his optimistic mindset, and he saw those harrowing years as a golden opportunity for future growth. He was constantly in touch with CEOs of various independent companies that he was doing business with, most of whom told him that many of their suppliers had cut down on sales forces to save money. He thought it was imperative to do the opposite and kept his entire sales team up and running as if nothing was out of the ordinary. They met to brainstorm regularly, laying down a firm plan of attack for how to navigate those tough times. Mr. Brown knew that the storm would pass in due time.

He told his team to venture out with confidence and to travel as much as they could, ideally every week. He was not expecting miracles, but he expected everyone to bring in enough sales to at least cover the cost of their travels. He challenged his sales team members to open at least two new accounts every week they traveled, no matter how small the sale was. He also encouraged them to stay positive. It was important to stay in attack mode against all odds.

To add to the drama, it was also a time when Mr. Brown's firm was at a tipping point. As I was writing this story, I asked him how he could remain so positive in a time of crisis and how he could be confident that they would reach their goals. He replied, "You know, when I landed on this soil, I came with nothing. I just had a strong will, raw determination and the desire to succeed. I had tremendous faith in this land of ours and it did not disappoint me. This recession is just a hurdle we can overcome. We just need to have patience and persistence and keep our heads on our shoulders. After all, if this great country goes under, the whole world will sink."

The team realized that his expectations were neither impossible nor unattainable. He wanted to boost their moral and show them that realistic dreams lead to positive vibrations. Everyone was pepped up and stepped up to the plate, including my friend Kow.

Kow was already a road warrior by then and entering his third year with the firm. He embraced Mr. Brown's strategy and started traveling quite aggressively, targeting the Midwest. He set his personal goals high and strategized about how to open as many new accounts as possible and sell nothing less than the minimum to cover his expenses. The strategy worked well but travelling was hard for the first few months. Kow would often find himself in tough spots and call Mr. Brown for some advice or, more often, for a positive-vibrations-recharge in the form of an encouraging pep talk. Sometimes he would call as late as 11:00 p.m. while driving to his next destination. Mr. Brown always picked up the phone.

During these adventures, Kow observed that many clients had a common problem; losing sales to big box brand stores. Even worse, they were losing sales on their basic bread and butter merchandise. Kow decided to do a simple S.W.O.T. analysis, which was something he picked up while attending the Krannert School of Business at Purdue University. While understanding one's strength it is important to be detached and 100% practical. Business is like a warzone. It's important to know your ammunition before you enter the battlefield. He charged ahead with this weapon and a positive attitude.

S.W.O.T – Strengths, Weaknesses, Opportunities, Threats

Strengths

The biggest strength that an independent retailer has is its' independence. It is this flexibility that allows them to be creative with their branding, merchandising, and marketing.

- They are a local neighbor. Their families shop at the local grocery store. Their kids go to the local school.
- They are active in the community, so consumers already know their faces. One can safely say they are part of the backbone of the town's prosperity.

- This comfortable feeling is the strongest value one can provide to a customer.

Weaknesses

While it is all about the right attitude, having a positive attitude is a must, there are some practical weaknesses that independents face.

- Since a lot of independent retailers are family owned, they tend to stick with old traditions instead of evolving and adapting quickly with the times. This lack of adaptation makes them out of date.
- Overwhelming marketing and promotions from big box brand competition causes them to worry so much that their sales team lacks the conviction to present their own products with genuine confidence. It is this lack of confidence that deters the retailer and sales team from explaining to the customer that they may not be the lowest in price, but they offer the best value in terms of quantity, price and service.
- Lack of capital, especially for marketing purposes, deters them from thinking rationally about how to evolve and grow their business.

Opportunities

When you look for opportunities, first look at your strengths and analyze how these strengths can help to open doors for opportunity. Similarly look at your weaknesses. Ask yourself what you can do to eliminate your weaknesses which can then pop open the door for opportunity.

- After visiting various stores in different towns, Kow realized independent retailers were missing a few categories of quality products at a price point that could compete with the big box brand stores. The single most important opportunity Kow found, was to create these product categories with value price points. He could then give this tool to the independent retailers, so they were not only able to compete with big box brand stores, but also able to make a decent profit for themselves.
- Opportunity will vary with the industry, the location and the country. Even within the same industry, opportunity varies with location.

Threats

- There are always threats when you have a thriving business.
- The trivial threats could be competitors stealing successful strategies.
- Big box brand stores trying to entice you to jump into a price war.
- The biggest threat of all to a retailer, is getting too comfortable and lazy once business becomes successful. They stop evolving and using their

> creativity. The easy way to avoid this threat is to never forget the joy of your craft.
>
> - Ironically, a threat to Kow's clients was also fellow independent stores in the same town. If the client he was talking to decide to do nothing and not try to stand out in tough times, then they would lose the opportunity to educate the customer about the differences in value and service they offered as an independent retailer compared to the big box brands and the other independent retailers.

To make use of the above analysis, it was very important to know what the competition was selling and at what price. By educating a client about what their competition was doing, they would be able to come up with a product that could compete. With those observations in mind, Kow started shopping around the stores in town and comparing pricing. He started compiling data for both the big box brand stores and the independent retailers.

After a careful review, he presented his findings to his fellow team members and clients. Kow identified a product quality that would be able to compete against the mass market. The product offered, could help the retailer make it through the recession with the right marketing plan. In fact, they were so confident that they offered a money back guarantee on this new promotion. All the sales team members got pepped up to use the same S.W.O.T. approach with their own clients in their respective towns.

In the end, the team had added over one hundred new accounts to their roster by helping the smaller retailers stay open and make a profit. After the storm had passed, these same new accounts and the already existing accounts became instrumental in increasing sales volume and taking Mr. Brown's firm to the next level.

Mr. Brown wanted his team to realize that this was not luck, nor an accident, nor chance that got them out of the mess of 2008-2009. They took initiative to go step by step, town by town and state by state to pave their own path out of the turmoil and negativity of that year. They knocked on the doors of prospective clients all over the country, looked adversity in the face, and said, "We will succeed."

THE WRAP UPS – BY MR. BROWN

- *Do not let fear stifle your growth.*
- *Fear is a great motivator when you run together instead of running away.*
- *When you find a true mentor, trust them with complete faith.*
- *Stay on the pulse of what service your customers need you to provide them and evolve.*

CHAPTER

PROPOSITIONED

Are you a good storyteller?

PROPOSITIONED

"Never let a good story go untold." – Mr. Brown

Wytheville, Virginia - November

You could say it was cold in Virginia, but it was nowhere near the kind of cold Mr. Brown was used to in New York. As always, he was dressed casually with a baseball cap on. Maybe that was why people looked at him like he was a bit out of place because he was not wearing a winter coat. Or maybe it was because he was clearly a visitor in the small Virginia town of Wytheville. After finishing his work for the day, our Mr. Brown asked his client Jamie if he would like to join him for dinner. Unfortunately, Jamie took a raincheck, having previous commitments with his family. Mr. Brown asked Jamie for a restaurant recommendation and he suggested Peking Chinese Restaurant about a five-minute drive from his office.

It was just a little after 5:00 p.m. when he reached the scenic location on top of a cliff. What a view! He parked his car, went inside, and was greeted by the hostess. The restaurant was all but empty since it was still early for dinner, so he did not feel bad requesting a spacious booth in which he could sit comfortably. As she escorted him, he took in the beautiful Chinese decorations, painted vases and wooden carvings. He took a seat, setting his backpack on the cushion across from him. The booth was perfect because he could keep an eye on the people coming in and out. Mr. Brown had a habit of observing the people around him while traveling, especially while carrying expensive merchandise in his bag.

A moment later, he felt someone's eyes on him. He glanced around and his gaze landed on a child around five who had probably been fed too much sugar. He was with his mother at a booth near the entrance and the mother was staring dead at Mr. Brown.

The waitress came over and blocked his view, breaking his paranoia and bringing his mind back to his stomach. He ordered a simple meal of steamed rice and spicy broccoli with extra ginger. While he was waiting for the food to arrive, he ventured a look back at the mother and saw that her eyes were still focused on him. It always made him uneasy when he caught someone staring, even though he had a habit of watching other people too. He started to squirm a little in his seat, hoping she would just finish her dinner and leave. After about ten minutes of this, he was relieved to see her asking for her bill. Excited to be out of the booth, her son moved to the center of the room, closer to him, and started playing on the floor.

He forgot about them as his food arrived. He realized just how hungry he was. The food there was just as good as his client had promised, the steaming rice and spicy broccoli piping hot in a garlic ginger sauce. His eyes were on his plate when all a sudden, the lady walked past her son and over to his table. "May I join you?" she asked. Mr. Brown stayed glued to his seat, frozen, not knowing how to respond. For a moment he felt suspicious and thought she must be setting him up. Why did she want to join him if she had already finished her dinner? What did she want with him, a total stranger? Something must be up!

Like a computer, his mind started to analyze every moment from the time he'd entered the restaurant until the food had hit the table. Was her husband outside waiting to grab his bookbag full of merchandise as soon as he leaves? Had they been following him since the meeting with his client?

As she waited for his response, he realized that it might be considered an insult in this small southern town to turn down her request. Mr. Brown took his backpack and moved it next to him as a precaution. "Please do join me," he told her. She made herself comfortable and quietly observed him as he continued to eat. Her son was still playing on the floor and she seemed like she had no intention of leaving anytime soon.

"You must be a traveler," she said, "I have never seen you here before."

"Yes, ma'am," was his simple answer.

Her eyes peered into his as if she were calculating something. "You are eating only rice and broccoli? No meat or chicken?"

"No, ma'am I don't," he replied. Now he was getting irritated because the vegetarian food was good and all he wanted to do was eat it in peace, but he wasn't about to talk with his mouth full.

She continued, "It is getting very cold outside. It's almost time for Thanksgiving dinner. You are welcome to stay with us! Our house is warm, and we will be happy to have you."

This was like a bomb going off in Mr. Brown's mind and he almost choked on his food. Was she propositioning him?

"You will be comfortable there," she continued. "You can have breakfast, lunch and a warm dinner. You are welcome to stay if you need to. It's no problem at all."

Not knowing what to say, he replied, "Okay, please give me the directions." He started eating again quickly, before his food got cold. Plus, the sooner he was out of there the better. Who knew what she was up to or what might be waiting for him outside?

The waitress came, interrupting their conversation. She smiled at the lady as Mr. Brown gave her his pen, asking her to write the directions on the back of the notepad. She wrote her name, number and address, then verbally gave directions, saying, “Go down the hill, cross the railroad tracks, come to the main street, turn left on the main street. After a few blocks there is a car dealership, turn left and on the next block you will see a white brick stone house and that’s where we live.” She then stood up and collected her son. Before leaving she said, “See you soon!”

The waitress came back over to clear his plate and a thought occurred to him. He figured most of the staff serving here must know the regular patrons. Also, the waitress had been speaking to the lady at her table for some time before she had decided to join him. Maybe she knew exactly what the woman was after. When the waitress returned with the check, he asked her if she knew the lady by showing her the name on the notepad.

“Oh, you mean the woman who was sitting next to you. Yeah, I know her. She’s a wonderful woman with a big heart. She helps our community a lot. Actually, she’s in charge of the only homeless shelter in town.”

He couldn’t help but laugh, feeling a little stupid. What a misunderstanding and a relief too! And what a wonderfully selfless way to help a stranger. Why had he let his mind wander off and get the best of him? He started thinking about it more and of course it all made sense. He was sitting there underdressed for the season and it was cold out for a native Virginian. The lady had noticed him eating only vegetables. She probably thought he couldn't afford meat or chicken, as there probably weren't too many vegetarians in Wytheville. Plus, he was carrying a large backpack. She must have been under the impression that he didn't have a car and was walking from place to place. She had only come over because she felt sorry for him and wanted to help him by offering warm shelter to sleep in and hot food to eat.

After Mr. Brown returned from his business trip, his family members and friends went out for dinner. He could not wait to tell them the story of his restaurant encounter. He told me how he could see all the ladies, especially his wife, glued to their seats wondering if he had stayed with another woman. You could hear a pin drop at the table even with all the commotion in the restaurant. Everyone was relieved when he revealed that the lady oversaw a homeless shelter!

Mr. Brown went on to tell the story to clients at restaurant meetings or on phone calls as well. Everyone loved the suspense and were curious to hear the end. When he reached the heartwarming ending, they had a big laugh and some even begged him to tell the story about that one time in Virginia to their friends. Those friends quickly became prospective clients. He would keep the conversation going by asking if anyone else would be that quick to help a stranger in town? Ultimately, this one anecdote helped Mr. Brown strike up conversations, open new doors, meet new people and increase his sales.

Are you a good storyteller? If not, you must practice! Storytelling is a craft that always comes in handy. Think of how many times a person you just met won you over because of how wonderfully that person told a story. By sharing a personal experience, you can easily break the ice, diffuse tensions in a room and make new friends. The possibilities are endless. You just need to be confident enough to tell your story.

THE WRAP UPS – BY MR. BROWN

- *Stop. Assess. Never jump to conclusions.*
- *The world is full of Good Samaritans who are willing to help a stranger.*
- *Storytelling is an art. Practice it.*
- *Do not underestimate the power of a good laugh in business.*

BE GENUINE

By Kaushal Shah

Have you ever realized that by trying to find the most convenient way to make our lives simpler and easier, we ironically end up making things more complicated? The same is true of how we operate our businesses.

With most complications, if we strip them down to the basics, we will find that they are not complicated at all. It does not require fabrication or complicated algorithms or system management software.

Being genuine is the right value that truly defines the experience that one should have with the client. We are giving it all to help the client. Being genuine comes with an educated solution alongside it. Your thoughts, your energy, your actions and your focus are directed towards fully answering the question of what ideas, resources and efforts are needed to find the solution to any problem.

Because of this, the client knows that when you commit to or promise anything to them, you have done the groundwork so they know that you care and that you genuinely can help them most of the time. The question here is how far and to what extent will you accept your client's challenges as your own? What is the best you can do to help them?

Sometimes helping them is beyond your means and control. In this context being genuine does mean having to say NO. It is practical and preferable to be honest and genuine by saying NO, rather than saying YES and risk losing a client's trust and confidence.

BE GENUINE

WHY THIS BOOK?

A Note from the Author

Why did I write this book? My dear reader, sometimes you meet someone that you can't quite shake. Something about Mr. Brown's character always stuck in my head like gum on the shoe. I graduated from Denison University with a BFA in Theatre and a Minor in Psychology, so long story short, I have always had an interest in how people think and how their characters develop. I found myself curious to find out more. Knowledge and education, I can always get from books, but it is not the same as what I can learn from someone's real life experiences. After learning so many lessons from someone, it is only natural to want to share that experience with others. Little did I know, Mr. Brown would propel me into my next season, my next level.

Let's backtrack. To pursue my dreams, I moved to New York City after college. I often found myself writing in the park, on the subway, on my phone at work, any time that an idea struck I always wrote it down. Unfortunately, I fell into a cycle of work because I had to survive in NYC, work to eat, work because I had to pay a high rent. Month after month the cycle repeated. Then, I started to get snags in my cycle. I encountered roommate issues and bills were adding up, so I had to add another job. Less time to do what I really came to the city to do and less time for hobbies like writing.

As I hopped from apartment to apartment, I found myself throwing my journals into boxes and letting them sit in the back of my closet, knowing I would be moving them again soon. When I finally settled into a much better apartment with my good friend Kow, it was finally time to unpack those boxes because I knew I would be there for at least a year.

Kow and I were both in our mid-twenties at the time and were trying to figure out our lives. Kow would come home from work and tell me some of the unbelievable stories about his mentor and what he did that sounded just plain crazy. Those encounters, some of which you read about, were crazy real encounters and they were helping Kow grow. When I met Mr. Brown, I saw just how much gumption he had to do what it took to please a client and grow a new friend.

Mr. Brown helped me realize that writing was a strong passion of mine. He and Kow were right. When I opened one of the boxes in the back of the closet, I hadn't realized just how much all my writing had added up over the years. Kow told me to come out of my Comfort Zone and start organizing the box and make something of these stories. I took his advice and started writing more actively. Coming out of the Comfort Zone was probably the most important lesson Kow had learned from Mr. Brown, but I had a long way to go.

Over the years, Kow's mentor became my mentor, shared with me his life story as well as the mistakes he made in business and of how he ended up here. Because of those experiences, I learned not to make the same mistakes and learned how important it was to take chances. He saved me from the frustrations of trial and error, wasted time and wasted money. Mr. Brown had used every adversity to his advantage. They made me truly realize just how lucky I was to have already been born into this golden land of opportunity, the United States of America. I could be anything I wanted to be and do anything I wanted to do, so why was I letting myself get caught up in this cycle?

I thought there must be many young entrepreneurs like me who would profit from these valuable lessons as well. These lessons learned can be true for anyone, anywhere, in any profession. I just had to share them with the world. I decided to write this book as my first step out of my Comfort Zone. Those stories gave me the guts to pursue my dreams and this book is my movement in that direction. I want to thank Kow and Mr. Brown for allowing me to share their experiences with a broad audience. Find that grit inside of you to fulfill your vision. Make your first move out of your Comfort Zone today!

Don't ever be under the impression that the great depression, the great recession or similar situations will not occur again in our lifetime. They will occur within one form or the other at some time in the future. You as an individual and/or entrepreneur will have to be mentally ready and be prepared to face this reality. Practical lessons learned and experiences earned can be put to the test and come in handy if the need arises.

Enjoy the ride that awaits you and don't ever settle or give up on your dreams!